Slaying Dragons

What Exorcists See
&
What We Should Know

2nd Edition
Revised and Expanded

Written by
Charles D. Fraune

Slaying Dragons:
What Exorcists See & What We Should Know

Charles D. Fraune, M.A.

2nd Edition

2019

Nihil obstat: Reverend Matthew Kauth, S.T.D.
                  Censor Deputatus

Slaying Dragons Press
www.TheRetreatBox.com
2019

Dedication

To Our Lady of Sorrows,
and to the glorious and triumphant Archangel,
Saint Michael.

For this purpose, the Son of God appeared, that He might destroy the works of the devil.

1 John 3:8

St. Michael the Archangel,
defend us in battle.
Be our protection
against the wickedness and snares of the Devil.
May God rebuke him, we humbly pray,
and do thou,
O Prince of the heavenly hosts,
by the power of God,
cast into hell Satan, and all the evil spirits,
who prowl about the world
seeking the ruin of souls.
Amen.

Table of Contents

Author's Note

This book relies on the wisdom and teachings of many exorcists who confront the devil and his demons as a central aspect of their priestly ministry. These experiences provide them with unique insights into the workings of the diabolical and the power of grace flowing from Our Lord Jesus Christ through His Holy Church. It is important to note, however, that while their teachings are uniquely insightful and beneficial to the faithful, exorcists are not speaking in an official capacity as representatives of the Magisterium of the Church. This book touches on some matters that have not been defined by the Church, but what is contained herein is not contrary to Church teaching.

In Gratitude

I am indebted to, and most grateful for, our faithful priests, for their generosity in tirelessly handing on the Sacred Traditions of our Holy Catholic Faith, and for working to ensure that the faithful in this age are taught the truths of prayer and spiritual warfare, and are thus fortified in this battle "against the principalities, against the powers, against the world rulers of this present darkness, against the spiritual hosts of wickedness in the heavenly places." (Eph. 6:12) Through all of our beloved priests who are truly dedicated to the salvation of souls, the faithful are encouraged to put on the "whole armor of God" (Eph. 6:13) and can find peace in the protective arms of the Church. May the Holy Spirit reward them and continue to bless their ministry.

Preface

Slaying Dragons is a book that I never expected to write. Though of interest to me at times throughout my life, matters like those within demonology were never things I pursued to any depth. As I look back now, it is a curious thing that the details of the spiritual war were never articulated to me, except in somewhat random conversations with priest friends. What brought me to the point of writing this book was purely Divine Providence. In my later years guiding high school students in the truths and realities of the Faith, spiritual warfare and exorcism details became more relevant to me. I followed this new sense of urgency and began my studies. Once that process began, I quickly knew that I, as a teacher and a writer, must go about turning all of this extraordinary spiritual wisdom into a book for others to more easily access.

This book addresses an aspect of the spiritual life of every Catholic which is delicate and vital to understand properly. While I am trained in the doctrine of the Faith, I am not an exorcist, nor have I assisted exorcists in any part of their ministry. Even were I interested, it seems that most exorcists prudently do not accept the assistance of laymen who are young or who still have children at home. That being said, I believe that Our Lord, through His Providence in my life, prepared me to take on the task of writing this book. After my return to the Faith, which I will describe briefly below, I pursued the priesthood for about nine years. In that process, I completed three internship years at different diocesan parishes, three semesters of seminary, and a ten-week intensive summer spiritual formation program. After discerning that Our Lord was not calling me to the priesthood, I began and completed a Master of Arts in Theology.[1]

---

[1] See "About the Author" for more details.

Those many years of my life led me to befriend countless priests from all areas of the East Coast, and to spend time with them, asking them everything I could think of regarding the life of a Catholic, uniquely broadening my grasp of our Faith.

This Present Book

This current book, in its Second Edition, has a long story which began with a study of the published lectures of Fr. Chad Ripperger. As far as I have noticed, there are more lectures and conferences available online from this exorcist than from any other exorcist in the country. As a result, I spent the better part of a year watching and studying every presentation I could find related to spiritual warfare. My original intent was to collect the wisdom of exorcists and saints and compile it into a book as part of a small Catholic business project that I was mulling over at the time.

Once I immersed myself in these teachings, I began to change my course. I felt compelled to not only share with my students everything I was learning, but also take my notes and organize them into a book. This I did, and it became a fascinating compilation of the teachings of this great exorcist. After seeing the appeal, and the need among the faithful for a book of this sort, I decided to greatly expand that original version and republish it as this Second Edition.

This present book, then, truly takes its inspiration from the teachings of Fr. Ripperger. These form the basic structure of the book. It was from a study of his teachings that I decided upon the layout of the book, including the major themes and Chapters, and the direction the material would take the reader.

The Second Edition keeps the original structure and builds upon it. This Edition no longer relies solely on one exorcist but incorporates the teachings of at least twelve exorcists and the writings of many saints and Doctors of the Church. As a result, this Edition is a deeper, richer, more thorough and comprehensive, and more insightful presentation of the same material as in the earlier edition.

One of the fruits of this additional labor is the evidence that Fr. Ripperger is not alone in his view of the spiritual battle in which we all find ourselves. Priests and bishops all over the world see exactly what he sees. In my research for this Second Edition, I kept remarking to myself, "They all say the same thing!" Though there are a few particulars over which exorcists debate, they agree on almost everything else. They also make it clear that the world of the diabolical is mysterious, and that exorcists rely on a community and network to support them and help them understand the best way to fight the demons and liberate souls from their grasps.

One fruit, among many, which this book may produce is a new appreciation and understanding of what exorcists are going through in this most important work for the salvation of souls. God is calling the Church to raise up more exorcists, but when a priest is called up by his Bishop, it is, more often than not, an up-hill battle to attain the knowledge and confidence he needs to fulfill this ministry.

The Present Author

A little background on the present author and my interest in the material covered in this book might be beneficial to share as these topics are not unrelated to my own life. I enjoyed a childhood that tended toward depression from a very young age and that culminated in a deep depression and acute anxiety in late high school and early college. This tendency toward depression, without a firm faith foundation, led me to often dwell on dark topics and dark thoughts, to the point of preferring stories that revolved around similar themes, such as evil, witchcraft, horror movies, and the diabolical. My birthday is the thirtieth of October and, during my youth, I enjoyed this fact because I felt it connected me to the dark culture attached to the modern celebration of Halloween. I never became a "gothic" person, thankfully, and my curiosity level was restricted by a strong sense of fear, so I never dabbled too deeply in the occult. Despite that, in my youth, I was more open to and curious about forbidden spiritual realities than I should have been.

At the worst moment in my descent into depression and anxiety, when I felt there was no deeper into misery that I could go, Our Lord interceded in a slightly miraculous way, and communicated to me that He had not abandoned me, contrary to what I had believed. As a result of that understanding, I returned to the practice of the Faith, which I had never thought much about prior to that moment and had casually abandoned for the year and a half following my graduation from high school. Just over a year after returning to the Faith, I was attending daily Mass and going to Confession regularly. As soon as I arrived at that point, where the Faith was now central in my life, and it was made clear to me that I must always remain in a state of grace, Our Lord began to bestow great favors upon me.

These great favors could be described in two themes: dreams and joy. As I reflect now, it seems that Our Lord was reconstructing my imagination with these two graces. For a decade and a half, I had allowed dark thoughts to occupy my daydreaming and imagination and these needed to be purged. The best way to do this, it seemed, was to flood my imagination with images of Our Lord's love in varying forms. The joy that accompanied this was like an intoxication by the Holy Spirit: there is no other way to describe it. The effect was a strong, abiding, vivifying, and elucidating peace, completely transforming me from the depressed and anxious person I had previously been. The closer I came to Our Lord in pious acts and concrete choices that anchored my salvation more deeply in Him, the more intense this joy would become. The joy led to a desire to constantly think of Our Lord, even to the point of truly being distracted by Him as I went about my day.

This supernatural preoccupation manifested in my dreams as well. These dreams, more often than not, had a prophetic nature to them, and have remained clear in my memory for the last eighteen years. They were so real and efficacious that I would often confuse them with memories from my daily life. They included, among other things, being in close friendship with the Apostles, with St. Francis of Assisi, numerous times with St. Pio of Pietrelcina, and numerous times with Our Lord and Our Lady. Each dream brought with it an understanding of the spiritual life and Our Lord's love, often accompanied by a particular grace that was necessary to my spiritual growth.

In addition to these, and relevant to this book, I experienced what I have always referred to as the "Devil dreams." These were a series of five or more dreams, over a period of three years, each spaced out by many months. Despite the time between them, each dream built upon the previous one, producing a single story in the end. Regardless of whether these dreams were from Our Lord or from the devil, they highlighted the fact that the evil one pursued me and sought to seduce me with promises of earthly power and success, but would also turn on me if I resisted his overtures.

With this being the manner of welcome which Our Lord gave to me as I returned to the Faith, the spiritual battle we are all in took a central place in my mind and interests. The journey from this point forward was arduous and eventful and led to a very protracted effort to arrive at seminary, which had consumed my desires from the first moments of my return to the Faith. After nine years, while finally in only my third semester of seminary, I clearly discerned that Our Lord did not want me to be a priest, contrary to what I had thought and wanted. Within four months of accepting this fact, and acting upon it, my life began to fall into place. I met the woman I would marry, embarked on the pursuit of my Master of Arts in Theology, started teaching at a Catholic middle school, and then was hired as the founding Theology teacher at a brand new Catholic High School.

It was during the last eight years in the latter position that I was providentially brought to a deeper study of the Church's teachings and the actual facts regarding spiritual warfare. My mind was now gaining the necessary clarity on a topic that had long been deeply relevant to me. As I learned more and more about this topic, I desired to share this with everyone. Given the rise in the rejection of the Faith and the acceptance of evil, it is critical that people know what is really going on in the spiritual and material realms. The spiritual battle is truly not confined to the invisible but manifests here in full force.

The Exorcists

Included in this book are the teachings and statements of the following exorcists, listed here in order of the frequency of their appearance in the book:

+ **Fr. Chad Ripperger**, priest and exorcist of the Archdiocese of Denver, Colorado, and founder of the Doloran Fathers. His apostolate also includes the organization *Sensus Traditionis*, where many of his conferences may also be found.
+ **Fr. Gabriele Amorth**, renowned Italian exorcist and founder of the International Association of Exorcists.

+ **Fr. Jose Antonio Fortea**, priest and exorcist of the Diocese of Alcala de Henares (Madrid), Spain.
+ **Fr. Gary Thomas**, priest of the Diocese of San Jose, California and exorcist whose training in Rome was the subject of the book, *The Rite: The Making of a Modern Exorcist* by Matt Baglio.
+ **Fr. Jeffrey Grob**, priest and exorcist of the Archdiocese of Chicago.

Additional exorcists referenced:

+ **Fr. Piero Catalano**, disciple of Fr. Amorth, and priest and exorcist of the Diocese of Reggio Calabria, Italy.
+ **Fr. Paolo Carlin**, priest and exorcist of the Diocese of Faenza-Modigliana, Italy.
+ **Fr. Randall Weber**, priest and exorcist of the Diocese of Salina, Kansas.
+ **Fr. Cesare Truqui**, priest and exorcist of the Diocese of Chur, Switzerland.
+ **Msgr. John Esseff**, priest and exorcist of the Diocese of Scranton, Pennsylvania, and founder of the Pope Leo XIII Institute.

Those who work in deliverance ministry:

+ **Fr. Carlos Martins**, priest of the Companions of the Cross and organizer of Treasures of the Church.
+ **Adam Blai**, layman, Peritus of religious demonology and exorcism for the Diocese of Pittsburgh, Pennsylvania.

Introduction

Anyone who is paying attention to spiritual matters at this time in the history of the world is aware that things are quite destabilized. The practice of the Christian Faith is dying in most parts of the world. The majority of Catholics do not believe the teachings of the Church and do not even attend Sunday Mass regularly. Many Catholics, in addition to many Protestant groups, are capitulating to the spirit of the world and embracing as good those acts which have always been seen as gravely immoral. Exorcisms, and a demand for them, are on the rise all throughout the world. In the US, the number of adherents of paganism and witchcraft have risen to figures surpassing the number of registered Presbyterians. Satanists feel quite comfortable being out in the open and U.S. laws have been proven powerless to stop the spread of this evil into the public sectors of our society.[1]

In the midst of this perfect storm, many Church leaders have demonstrated themselves to be unwilling to teach the fullness of the Church's traditions in matters of belief and practice. As a result, most Catholics do not believe, or even think twice about, the existence of the devil or spiritual warfare, even though Sacred Scripture is filled with references to this aspect of our spiritual lives. Further, due to the rising number of Catholics who live and remain in a state of mortal sin,[2] exposure to the influence of the diabolical is extremely high. These Catholics, though, are completely unaware of the spiritual danger they are in, and of the weapons they can use to protect themselves and combat the demons that pursue them.

Despite this ignorance, priests who have maintained the sacred traditions of our Faith are making use of modern means of communi-

---

[1] Covered in Chapter Eleven
[2] Due to the widespread laxity in the practice of the Faith, esp. Mass attendance, Confession, and sexual morals.

1

cation to proclaim all of the liberating truths that the faithful need to know. Of particular interest to us here, in this book, is the work of the many exorcists who have given to the faithful countless talks, conferences, and books on spiritual warfare and exorcisms and have permitted those to be available on the internet in audio and video formats. Compiling the teachings of at least twelve exorcists and many saints and Doctors of the Church, this book conveys the critical matters of spiritual warfare, in both teaching and practical application, for the instruction of laymen who desire to know more about the intricacies of our battle with Satan and his demons.

The activity of demons is often dismissed as something on which we should not focus. While this is true in the sense of avoiding an obsession with this dark topic, it is false if it causes us to avoid attributing anything, relative to our spiritual lives, to the work of demons. It is a fact of our holy Faith that demons pursue us and seek to subtly lead us away from God, in ways that are often difficult for us to detect. They are one of the three sources of temptation: the world, the flesh, and the devil. The fallen world is an institution of evil, which broadcasts its own maxims and philosophies and pulls men away from the worship of God. Our flesh is fallen and wounded and inclined, through concupiscence, toward sin and a rejection of God out of a preference for self. The demons are real, personal beings who freely chose to reject God and are now fixated on opposing everything that is good, in particular His effort to save mankind with His mercy.

When we are tempted, we are tempted on several levels: by the prevailing beliefs of our family and friends and society at large, by our flesh with its disordered cravings and irrational choices, and by the demons who have studied us and seek to encourage our faults and weaknesses. In this storm of temptation, the Church shines as a beacon of Truth and clarity and freedom. The light that she transmits to the world scatters the demons, illuminates the intellect, and purifies the flesh. Not only in her teachings, but also in her Sacraments and sacramentals, the Church gives to man what is needed to break free from the dominion of evil, both internally and externally.

Unfortunately, in this age of the Church, much that was once treasured and placed as a fixture in Catholic life has been lost and forgotten. This includes not only the wisdom of the spiritual masters, but also the knowledge and prudence to have recourse to the sacramentals that aid us in our battle. Following Our Lord's example, and heeding His commands and those of His Mother, the Church blesses certain natural things and sets them aside for sacred use. This includes, among other things, water, salt, oil, crosses, candles, rosaries, medals, images, statues, incense, and palm leaves. These items are given blessings which promise powerful effects to the faithful who use them with faith and devotion. Sadly, so few Catholics have heard of these and fewer still are the ones who actually use them and incorporate them into their lives.

Some may wonder what the benefit is of knowing what happens inside an exorcism. While, for some, it might be a bit creepy, it is important to know what demons are capable of doing. The demons that are manifesting and speaking directly through the possessed person to the exorcist are the same demons that whisper invisibly into our intellects to seduce us to sin. Those demons desire to push us, slowly, craftily, subtly, until we commit a mortal sin. At that point, they seek to dig their black talons into our flesh and remain with us. Ultimately, they are seeking to possess us, though, as the reader will learn, God only rarely permits them to do so. Demons will then settle for what is called diabolical obsession, where they are able to enter into the intellect in a powerful way, and bombard the person with a variety of thoughts, all intended to drive the person away from God.

The presence and persistence of the evil one and his many legions is not a debated issue among the faithful in the Church today. It is recognized far and wide that diabolical activity is on the rise, both in the fact that people are aligning themselves more with Satanism and witchcraft, and in the fact that more and more people are being forced to seek out exorcists for deliverance and liberation.

Know your enemy. Know his tactics. Know his motives. Know his nature. Know his origin. Know his goal. Know his language. Know his network. Know his strengths. Know his weaknesses. Once this knowledge is obtained, you can more effectively predict your enemy's behavior, recognize his traps, use the proper preventative measures against him, and drive him away when he persists.

What will be of the greatest use to Catholics is the wisdom to know how to protect their spiritual lives from these aggressive and, literally, hell-bent demons.

Chapter One

The Motivation and Tactics of Demons

Our Lord is the King over all creation, including the angelic world. As a result, demons are only able to do those things which Our Lord permits them to do. However, like us, demons are creatures with an intellect and a free will and can choose the manner in which they initially and, to a certain extent, continuously rebel against God. They are also capable of designing their own attack protocols as they seek to drag mankind into Hell with them.

Exorcists learn much of what they know from the time they spend interacting with demons within exorcisms. Demons will talk and exorcists have recounted that they can even get the demons to talk to one another during an exorcism. As exorcists have learned, demons will work together toward their goal, not out of a sense of fraternity but only since they have a common hatred of God. It is often the case that a person is possessed by more than one demon at the same time. The exorcist will then carefully listen in order to discover hints regarding the weaknesses of the demon(s) and use that against them in the process of liberating the person.

When there are multiple demons, they are in a hierarchical order, much like a military unit. As the exorcism successfully progresses, the weaker demons will leave first, but the higher demon will seek to remain.[1] A weaker demon will leave to avoid the suffering of the exorcism. Sometimes the demon will even make it clear to the exorcist that it was not the exorcist who cast him out but that he left only because he wanted to leave.[2]

---

[1] Amorth, 68-9
[2] Fortea, 109

It is critical to understand the motivation within the demons: pride, possessiveness, and vengeance. In their undying pride, the demons have lost all good things from God, and have rejected God in a manner that is irrevocable and beyond forgiveness. As Fr. Jose Antonio Fortea, has seen, "The capacity to love has been annihilated in the psychology of a demon."[3] Contrary to the demons, man, in God's mercy, has been offered repentance within this life. The refusal to offer mercy to the demons is "not a defect in the infinite divine mercy" but points to the "irrevocable character of their choice."[4] St. John Damascene states, "There is no repentance for the angels after their fall, just as there is no repentance for men after death."[5]

As a result, the demons resent men even more and wish to bring us all into Hell to suffer in the same manner as is their own punishment. Their initial evil motivations, which caused their Fall, are many and include such things as a disgust at the Incarnation and a refusal to submit to the Blessed Virgin Mary as their Queen.[6] There is no love within the demons, and their wills are completely set against truth.[7] Fr. Fortea says, "A demon's heart only hates; it revels in the suffering of others."[8] There is, however, much intelligence within the demons and they know our weaknesses well. It is our task to wage war against them and realize that they will not stop seeking our ruin until our souls have departed for Judgment.[9]

Demons possess people for one reason: to cause suffering. They take the risk that a possession may, in the end, make the person holier, because they desire so much to see that person suffer.[10] Since they are fallen from grace, they do not possess virtue, which would make them think twice about possessing a person. As Fr. Ripperger describes, demons will often be baited into a possession that Our Lord knows will only humiliate the demon and sanctify the person in-

---

[3] Fortea, 18
[4] CCC 393
[5] Ibid.
[6] Ripperger #5
[7] John 8:44
[8] Fortea, 18
[9] The popular blogger, Fr. Z, likes to compare the networking of demons to the NSA. If the NSA can collect as much information as we know they can, imagine how much more the demons can collect.
[10] Fortea, 18

volved. But the demon can't resist.[11] They are enslaved to their wills, which are fixed in the evil they chose, and they seek the immediate gratification from the harm they can inflict.[12]

While they are much smarter than we are, "The intellects of the rebellious angels were deformed and darkened by the very reasons they used to justify the rebellion of their wills against God."[13] St. Thomas Aquinas says that "although they are darkened by privation of the light of grace, yet they are enlightened by the light of their intellectual nature."[14] In discussing the intellects of the demons, it is fascinating to think about the fact, as Fr. Fortea mentions, that demons are not tempting us at every moment. "Much of the time," he says, "they spend thinking."[15] Since they still perceive the order of the world as set forth by the Creator, the thinking of the demons often leads to suffering when, inevitably, "their ponderings lead them to think about God."[16]

The demons know that they are damned and that they will be condemned and chained in Hell at Judgment Day. In Hell, though, they will pour out their wrath on all the inhabitants of that miserable abode. St. Alphonsus Liguori states that, at our Judgment, the devil will be the first one to come forward to accuse us. Quoting St. Augustine, he says the devil "will charge us before our face with what we have done, he will state the day and the hour in which we have sinned."[17] This will be the culmination of the works of Satan and his demons. Throughout our lives, they seek to lay traps for us and trip us. They hold every fault against us and lay it upon us in order to crush us with guilt.

In order to accomplish this, they offer worldly goods to us in exchange for our consent to sin and to reject God. This can happen in very common and hidden ways, such as through the general allure of the world and its many delights. It can also happen in the stage of diabolical temptation called subjugation, which is freely chosen by

---

[11] Ripperger #7
[12] Fortea, 84
[13] Fortea, 8-9
[14] Summa I, Q64, a1
[15] Fortea, 15
[16] Fortea, 15
[17] *Preparation for Death*, 244

the individual.[18]   Many in Hollywood have embraced the devil's promises in this manner, with some suspecting Bob Dylan,[19] who spoke in such a way in a TV interview, as well as John Lennon.[20] In the end, and even in this life, if the individual goes against their pact with the demon, the demon will eventually turn on the one whom they have deceived, because the devil is a liar, and the father of lies.[21]

Since the demons are creatures, they are ultimately weak in comparison with God and are under God's dominion just as is every other thing that God has created. They are permitted to carry out their deeds as part of God's plan, and only according to God's plan. This is part of God's permissive will, where He tolerates an evil in order to bring, through it, a much greater good.[22] Therefore, they are much more restricted than they would want to be and than we tend to think they are. According to St. Thomas Aquinas, a man's guardian angel is more powerful than even the Devil himself. This is due to the power of grace, which was granted to the holy angels after the test that accompanied the first instance of their existence. This can also be understood when reflecting on the holiness of the Blessed Virgin Mary. By nature, she is inferior to the angels. By grace, she is the Queen of the Angels and the demons run in fear at the mere mention of her name.[23]

The demons are not in possession of the kind and amount and depth of knowledge as are the angels who are faithful to the Lord. Sometimes our fear of the demons leads us to forget this detail. This knowledge is related to the gift of sanctifying grace and the possession of glory, which the demons lost in their rejection of God. The holy angels are already in the state in which we will be should we merit Heaven. This is why even our Guardian Angels are more powerful than the Devil. Furthermore, as exorcists attest, when demons manifest in the people they are possessing, they often do so in animalistic manners.[24] They are stuck in a deficient state, in a reduced state,

---

[18] Ripperger #3

[19] See page 160.

[20] See page 46. Exorcists see this reality often. Examples are given throughout the book.

[21] John 8:44.

[22] Romans 8:28

[23] *Glories of Mary*, 120, referencing St. Bonaventure.

[24] See page 19 for an example.

in a state that lacks the dignity proper to them as angelic beings. The number assigned to the Beast in the Book of Revelation, 666, reflects this permanent imperfection, as it is just below 777, which is a trinity of perfection, numerically speaking.

The Fall of the Demons

When the demons fell, they each did so in a manner that involved a rejection of Christ for one reason or another. It is the common theological belief that the angels, in the first moment of their existence, were tested in their fidelity to God and the plan which God had for the created world. According to St. Louis de Montfort, Satan fell as a result of the revelation of the perfection of the Blessed Virgin Mary,[25] who gained through humility what he lost through pride. As he says in one of his hymns, speaking for the devil who rages against the elect, "I am outraged, I am furious…for this soul has inherited what I lost in Heaven."[26] This perfection would place her above all the Angels, including Satan himself. Therefore, he would not only have to serve God but Our Lady as his Queen. Other demons rebelled and fell by principally opposing the mercy which Christ would show to mankind.[27]

Each individual spirit directly perceived and clearly understood God's revelation. It came to them immediately and with perfect clarity. This kind of intellectual perception is far superior to that of man. There was no delay in their response. As St. Thomas says, "The devil sinned at once after the first instant of his creation."[28] The spirits knew what it meant to say "yes" or "no" to God's revelation. All of these factors made the decision of these spirits permanent. Each spirit was assigned a duty to fulfill, and it was this that they either accepted or rejected. This is the sin that caused their fall, and which is also depicted in their names.[29] This sin also inspires their behavior which makes the knowledge of this sin one of the exorcist's key weapons.

---

[25] Ripperger #3

[26] St. Louis de Montfort, *Hymns,* 127:74

[27] Ripperger #3

[28] Summa, I, Q. 63, a6

[29] Ripperger #3

All of the spirits were created in an order within a hierarchy. There are nine choirs of spirits, the greatest being the choir of Seraphim, which means "burning ones," who stand in the presence of God such that they burn with the glory that He possesses. The least of the spirits are those in the choir of Angels. St. Thomas teaches that our Guardian Angels are taken from this choir.[30] The fall of the spirits resulted in empty thrones in the hierarchy of grace, which God intends to fill with the saints, whose degrees of holiness determine where in the order of grace they will be placed. This is the number of the "elect" whom Christ will save by the shedding of His Precious Blood. The saints will essentially replace the demons in this hierarchy.[31] This also helps to explain the vitriol with which specific demons act against us, since they know that, if we are saved, we will "steal" the throne that had first been offered to them.

Organization

As would be no surprise once you learn that the spirits were created in a hierarchy, the demonic realm can be described as operating like an organized "crime network," so to speak. According to Fr. Ripperger, exorcists have discerned through their work that under Satan there is a council of five demons who execute his commands. These are Baal, Asmodeus, Lilith, Leviathan, and Baphomet. The sins which are attributed to these five demons are fornication, homosexuality, and abortion, which are firmly settled in our culture.[32] He says that many possessions come about through these sins. As will be discussed in the last Chapter, Baphomet is the demon which modern Satanists are giving particular attention.[33]

This demonic network is one of three things that Fr. Fortea says demons spend most of their time focused on. In addition to delving deeper into knowledge and tempting people, demons also have relationships among themselves. These relationships are, of course, not secured by bonds of love, but the demons do find a certain amount of

---

[30] Summa 1, Q. 113, A 3
[31] "equality with angels is promised to the saints." Summa 1, Q.62, A 5
[32] Ripperger #11. See page 101 for a few more details.
[33] See page 161.

pleasure in these communications and in the shared work of tempting mankind.[34] Regarding possessions, stronger demons can control lower demons and prevent them from leaving a possession even if the lower demons are suffering and want to leave.[35]

Fr. Ripperger says that demons are extraordinarily sensitive to how they are perceived by other demons. During exorcisms, when the demon is losing his hold on the possessed and is about to be cast out, it often acts in a way that reveals it is worried about the humiliation and ridicule it will endure from the other demons. He says they are more worried about this than they are of the pain they endure from the rite of the exorcism itself.[36] This reflects what Fr. Fortea says, that demons have "real complex social relationships."[37]

The attack method is also quite organized as well. Fr. Ripperger teaches that, whereas God assigns an additional Guardian Angel to a validly married family, Satan seems to also assign a demon to tempt it.[38] Fr. Gary Thomas also speaks about Satan assigning demons to people.[39] However, we must remember that the Angel is on a permanent assignment given to him by God Himself. The demon assigned by Satan is there out of a spirit of rebellion against God. As a result, the demon can be removed, unless God allows the demon to remain, despite, as we see in the case of St. Paul, the prayers and protests of the holy family, or holy person, that it afflicts.[40]

When demons target a family or a person, a stronger demon will send a weaker demon first, to start to break into the family or the person's life. Once this has been successful, the stronger demon will arrive.[41] This is similar to what Our Lord said about the return of the demon once it is cast out of a man. After it wanders around, it returns to try to repossess the man. If that is not possible, it summons seven demons stronger than itself to complete the task.[42]

---

[34] Fortea, 12
[35] Fortea, 10
[36] Ripperger #6
[37] Fortea, 12
[38] Ripperger #7
[39] Thomas #2
[40] Cf. 2 Cor. 12:7-8
[41] Ripperger #8
[42] Matthew 12:45

Demons also tend to cling to families and move through the family line. This is called a generational spirit. Sacred Scripture points to these spirits at different moments in both the Old and the New Testament. In the Old Testament, for example, we see reference made to the Lord permitting a punishment on the children of the guilty father down "to the third and the fourth generation."[43] We see this generational spirit manifest in such passages as the story of the boy who is presented to Our Lord by his father.[44] The father states that the demon has bothered the boy "from childhood." St. Thomas relates St. Bede's comment on this passage as stating, "For what was there in the boy, that he should be troubled from infancy with a cruel devil, if he were not held at all by the chain of original sin?"[45] The boy is troubled "from infancy" by a demon as a consequence of original sin. St. Louis de Montfort alludes to this reality in his description of the effects of Eve's disobedience. He says, "By obeying the serpent, Eve ruined her children as well as herself and delivered them up to him."[46]

Fr. Ripperger says that these spirits can also dedicate themselves to a certain family for many generations, or to a cultural generation (like the 'hippies'), or to a country in an intellectual way (like Nazi Germany).[47] Fr. Gabriele Amorth said in an interview that the devil can possess groups of people, not just individuals. He said, "For example, I am convinced that the Nazis were all possessed by the devil. If you think about what types [of evil] like Stalin, Hitler did … certainly they were possessed by the devil."[48]

Guiding Principles

Despite rejecting all that is good and holy, demons still have principles which they hold dear.[49] The first and primary one, about which Fr. Ripperger states they are intensely scrupulous, is "anything

---

[43] Exodus 20:5. As a balance of God's mercy to this passage, read Deut. 7:9.

[44] Mark 9:21

[45] *Catena Aurea* – Gospel of Mark, Chapter 9

[46] *True Devotion*, 53

[47] Ripperger #8

[48] https://catholicherald.co.uk/prominent-exorcist-who-criticised-harry-potter-and-yoga-dies-at-91/

[49] Ripperger #6

but God." This principle is the exact opposite of the principle that must guide those who desire to become saints, which, according to St. Alphonsus, must be "Let all be lost, provided God is not lost."[50] The spiritual advice that Fr. Ripperger gives is to not spend so much time thinking about and analyzing yourself and your sin but, instead, to think about God as much as possible. As the exorcist Msgr. John Esseff states, "Sin is far worse than Satan."[51] It is our disconnect from God that leads us to rely on ourselves, which necessarily leads to sin and the loss of God.

Demons also treasure the idea "anything but moderation."[52] This is why demons will drive people to behaviors of extremes, whereas virtue is the mean between the two. Fr. Ripperger says that, for a sinful man, this will be a temptation to over-indulgence in the use of a good of this world. For someone seeking to eradicate an unhealthy attachment to something, instead of moderating the use of that worldly good, demons will drive people to total abstinence from it. As Fr. Ripperger further explains, God receives glory when we enjoy the things He has made. The demons envy what we have and want to steal away all the joys we can find in this world. So, they push us away from any sort of moderation and toward either over-indulgence or total abstinence. What we need, at all times, is virtue. Virtue, as its literal meaning implies, is a powerful tool for our health and sanctity.

Demons are also guided by the principle of division. As Fr. Amorth says, "Wars and the division of souls are unequivocal signs of the presence of the devil, which, not by chance, in Greek means 'divider'."[53] They seek, through every possible means, to divide: through manipulation of how we perceive others, through the lie stating that others may have bad motives toward us, and through temptation to sinful behaviors that result in our isolation from other people. In the end, the demons seek to create wounds. As Fr. Thomas says, demons are always looking for people with broken

---

[50] *Preparation for Death*, 322

[51] http://www.ncregister.com/blog/armstrong/exorcist-says-this-problem-is-far-worse-than-satan

[52] Ripperger #6

[53] Amorth, 124

relationships or no relationships.[54] The demons then pour their venom into these wounds to push us into a downward spiral from which they hope we will not emerge. Exorcists warn that too many people, at this point, reach out to mediums and witches and other occult avenues before seeking out a priest. This plays right into the game of the demons, in which they seek to create in us the same emotions that they themselves feel.

Demons will also, for this purpose, orchestrate external events in a person's life in order to bring harm upon that person, thus creating a wound, through which the demons can get a better hold on the person. In this wound, and through this hold, the demon gains power over them. This is why healing of the soul is important for spiritual growth. The wounds that have built up through sins, or through a life of sin, are the targets of the demons.[55] Once these are bound and healed, the demons have to take more advanced approaches against us. We must remember – the demons want us to fall into sin, and to die in a state of sin, and then to be subjected to them in Hell. We must know and accept this and do the work to avoid letting them win.

Beginning with Eve

The attacks of the diabolical began with the first man and woman whom God created, Adam and Eve, and specifically with Eve. Here we see the tactic of the devil to divide a family and create false perceptions in the mind. Fr. Ripperger points out that Satan suggested to Eve's emotions and her imagination, and placed images in her mind to stir up a perception that was not in harmony with reality.[56] The tactic was to put a twist on what God actually said and spin it to appear negative when it is actually positive. As a result, pride and desire were stirred within Eve and she broke the commandment and ate from the forbidden tree.

This is a common approach, and one for which we must always be watchful, and which we must use humility to defend against. It is easy for the demons to make us think one thing when the reality is

---

[54] Thomas #1
[55] Ripperger #10
[56] Ripperger #2

another. This ultimately, as with Eve, encourages us toward pride, which can also be called willfulness or self-will, as St. Alphonsus names it. St. Alphonsus quotes St. Augustine as saying, "The devil has been made a devil by self-will." He concludes then that, "when we do our own will, the enemy ceases to combat us; because then our wills are devils."[57] Once the devil turned Eve toward self-will, he could sit back and watch the consequences play out.

Eve also sinned through curiosity. Adam and Eve, as St. Thomas states, were gifted with natural integrity and perfection, and an intellect that possessed the knowledge of all things, such as the nature of all animals.[58] By this knowledge, as Fr. Ripperger points out, Eve would have known that there were no talking snakes in creation.[59] However, her curiosity regarding this strange creature led her to listen to Satan and follow his lead. As a result, she placed herself under him and gave him authority to act in her life.[60] Since Adam followed her lead, bringing about the Fall of Man, the demons can now physically act upon all of us, connected to Adam and wounded as we all are through original sin.

Affecting the Physical World

As a result of Adam and Eve following the lead of Satan, and obeying him, while rejecting God's command, the devil and his demons gained a certain amount of influence over the physical world. In the Gospel of John, Our Lord refers to Satan as the "prince of this world."[61] St. Thomas says that this, of course, is the devil, but that the devil's power is not a natural power, but one that comes from guilt. St. Thomas says, "He is not the ruler of creatures, but of sinners and darkness."[62] As Job states, "he is king over all the children of pride."[63] This rule, though, can impact even the good, such as Our Lord Himself. Though Satan has no true power over Christ, he has

---

[57] *True Spouse of Christ*, 143-144
[58] Summa 1, Q. 94, A 3
[59] Ripperger #3
[60] Ripperger #3
[61] John 14:30 DR
[62] Aquinas, Commentary, John 14
[63] Job 41:34 DR

influence over the sinful Judas, whom he incites to betray Christ, and over the sinful Jewish leaders, whom he incites to kill Christ.

Satan's activity can thus extend out from normal temptations and impact external aspects of human life. One of these is referred to as diabolical infestation. This is the term used to refer to external manifestations of demonic activity in the world. This can involve things like animals, as is depicted in Sacred Scripture in the story of the Legion of demons being sent into the pigs, who then ran madly off the cliff and plunged into the sea.[64] Fr. Ripperger relates a story about a house infested with a demon of illness which was brought into the house by a witch who lived there. She had attempted to heal her husband through a spell, but she ended up killing him instead, and introducing the demon into the house. A family later moved in there and found the house to be infested due to the sin of the witch. The demon who infested the house attacked the lower level of creatures first, eventually causing the death of two dogs in the home, due to the length of time it took to rid the house of the demon.[65]

The effects of infestation can be so disturbing that they can lead to economic impacts on the family affected. It can impact not simply the house, but also electrical appliances and automobiles. Windows opening and shutting, appliances turning on and off, voices and cries, repulsive noises, foul odors, abundant insects, pounding on the walls, and footsteps, are all signs of infestation. These, of course, will manifest without any natural explanation.[66] A demon, with God permitting, can also "move things at will" and cause objects to fly around the room or disappear and reappear somewhere else.

Infestations can result from "a hex, spell, or curse, or from voodoo or witchcraft."[67] Fr. Ripperger says that demons can also gain power in a space by acts such as blasphemy, which gives them a certain power over the air in that place.[68] You can tell an object is infested if the phenomena occur wherever the object is placed. Fr. Fortea advises that, "in such cases, the object must be burned after

---

[64] Mark 5:9ff
[65] Ripperger #3
[66] Amorth, 26, 74
[67] Fortea, 99
[68] This is one reason the Church blesses candles. See page 138. See page 163 for more on blasphemy.

being sprinkled with holy water. The ashes should then be buried"[69] or scattered in a stream.[70] Priests who are aware of the true spiritual battle that we are in are more than willing to take these items and destroy them for us.[71]

This activity of the demonic can have a terrible impact on the emotions and mental health of a person or a family. In Pennsylvania, a house was infested by a demon for nearly a century, and events such as were just mentioned had become commonplace. The Cranmer family eventually moved in and, with the help of the Church, the demon was expelled, but not before the manifestations tortured and psychologically wounded the family in a grave way.[72] According to Fr. Ripperger, diabolic infestation is becoming much more common today. He recommends inquiring about your neighbors and previous residents in your home, to see if extra spiritual protection or deliverance might be necessary.[73] Given that demons can essentially infest any inanimate item, it is a good and prudent thing, especially today, to receive all of the blessings, such as for cars and homes, that the Church provides.[74]

Demons cannot only impact the physical world external to man, but also some aspects of man internally. Demons can produce visions and false ecstasies, for example. St. Thomas states that "a demon can work on man's imagination and even on his corporeal senses, so that something seems otherwise than it is."[75] Demons can directly form an image in a man's imagination. This can be in the course of normal temptations or in the course of deceiving someone to think they are having a vision of the supernatural. This relates to another item that is within the reach of demons: apparitions. This is why the Church is so careful in investigating supposed apparitions; demons can simulate all of these things.[76] As a result, the Church waits to hear what the

---

[69] Fortea, 101

[70] Ripperger #3

[71] This might be helpful given the power that certain items can have in our lives. See page 112 for a related story.

[72] *The Demon of Brownsville Road*, by Bob Cranmer and Erica Manfred.

[73] Ripperger #4

[74] The traditional Roman Ritual has blessings for many items that people use, both in common life and for devotions.

[75] Summa 1, Q. 114, A 4

[76] Ripperger #3

content of the message is before deciding on the supernatural nature of the message. The reaction of St. Bernadette to the appearance of the Blessed Virgin Mary will serve us well to remember: she sprinkled holy water at the apparition and commanded it to depart if it was not from God.

As Fr. Ripperger describes, demons can also cause the perception of rays of light and heat and pleasant sensations.[77] They can appear to bring cures by simply removing an illness that is demonic in origin. They can also cause other bodily phenomena and simulate miracles such as levitation[78] and speaking in tongues. Fr. Fortea says, along with Fr. Ripperger, that, yes, a demon can also cause the stigmata. For Fr. Fortea, he originally did not believe this was possible until his experiences demonstrated otherwise. He learned that the origin of this phenomenon, since it can be caused by God or by a demon, must be discerned by the accompanying signs in the person's life, whether there is an increase of grace and virtue, or of sin and disobedience.[79]

Demons are also permitted to affect people in what is called vexation, or dolor, which is from the Latin for 'pain.' God has permitted that certain saintly people be allowed to be accosted or, essentially, beaten up by the demons. This is a physical assault, by an invisible person, on the saint while they live here on the earth. Fr. Ripperger says this is permitted for two reasons: for the continued sanctification of the person, in order to build greater confidence in God; and to humiliate the demon who, despite the attacks and beatings, is still unable to get the saint to give in and distrust God, reduce his prayer life, fall away from virtue, and sin.[80] There are numerous examples of these saints in the life of the Church, such as St. Pio of Pietrelcina (Padre Pio) and St. John Vianney (the Cure of Ars). A Scriptural example is Job, whom Our Lord permitted to be attacked by Satan in very intense ways. St. Augustine states the source of Job's sufferings quite plainly: "when fire came down from heaven and at one blow consumed

---

[77] Ripperger #3

[78] Applying the logic of St. Thomas, when anyone levitates, it is by the power of an angel. This applies to a saint and to an evil man or a possessed person. In the former, it would be a holy angel; in the latter, it would be a demon.

[79] Fortea, 118

[80] Ripperger #6

Job's servants and sheep; when the storm struck down his house and with it his children – these were the work of Satan, not phantoms."[81]

Demons are also permitted to manifest in visible forms. While demons are capable of appearing to us in any human form, God does not typically allow them to appear in any form they choose. Typically, as Fr. Fortea says, they "are permitted to appear as moving shadows, as monstrous freaks, or as very black, little men."[82] His description matches the experience of the Cranmer family mentioned earlier. Adam Blai, Peritus of religious demonology and exorcism, who also helps train exorcists, adds that these shadowy forms can be "the size of a mouse, a basketball, a child, an adult, or larger." They will be solid forms that can appear to walk or "float as a kind of rolling black smoke that does not dissipate."[83] A story was related to me of two teenagers who were playing with a Ouija board in an upstairs room when a tall dark figure suddenly appeared in the doorway before disappearing again. The next day, these individuals were driving on a highway when the same dark figure appeared in the middle of the road. The driver swerved to avoid the figure, careened off the road, and crashed. One individual was unharmed and the other was paralyzed.

The devil can appear as a "monstrous animal" or a person with satanic characteristics. He can also appear in innocent forms, as he did in the life of St. Pio. To this saint, the devil appeared as a ferocious dog, a naked girl, Our Lord, Our Lady, Padre Pio's confessor, and the father guardian of his monastery. Padre Pio was given an order from the latter and only realized it was actually the devil after he sought to verify what he had been told.[84] St. Teresa of Avila, in her autobiography, reports several times of witnessing an apparition of a little man, completely black, and snarling at her.[85]

While these things can sound intimidating, it is important to remember that they are only possible insofar as God permits the demons to act in these ways. Thus, all of these activities are permitted within

---

[81] Summa 1, Q. 114, A 4, quoting St. Augustine De Civ. Dei, XX, 19.
[82] Fortea, 115
[83] Blai, 42
[84] Amorth, 26
[85] *Life of Teresa*, 173

the divine plan for the salvation of souls and, as we will discuss more, the humiliation and defeat of the demons.

Curiosity

Curiosity can be a sinful act of the mind, and lead to an opening up to the diabolical when we, by this curiosity, stray from virtue, enter near occasions of sin, or dabble with things that are condemned by God and the Church. St. Alphonsus Liguori describes how curiosity can lead one, as in the case of Adam and Eve, to place oneself in a situation where a strong temptation will come against us. He says, "The neglect of avoiding the occasions of sin was the cause of the fall of our first parents. God had forbidden them even to touch the forbidden fruit. *God commanded us,* said Eve, *that we should not eat, and that we should not touch it.* But through want of caution she *saw, took, and ate it.* She first began to look at the apple, she afterward took it in her hand, and then ate it. He who voluntarily exposes himself to danger, will perish in it."[86]

One impact of curiosity, pertinent to the topic of this chapter, is the diabolical infestation of a home or dwelling. Infestation is, essentially, when the demons get into the home and stay there. This comes about as a result of some evil deed done inside the home or from a curse placed on the home.[87] Fr. Ripperger recounts a story involving a group of paranormal researchers whose investigation uncovered demonic activity inside a house. The group called a priest, who took care of the issue in the house. Fr. Ripperger was also involved at this point, perhaps as a consultant to that priest. The group was told that their initial curiosity was a great danger and that, by the time they discover demonic activity, it is too late. It is good to call the priest then, but they are already being targeted by the demon. In this situation, Fr. Ripperger said he could tell that the head of this group was already possessed. Exorcists, he states, from their experience and training, can often detect a certain look in a person that reveals this diabolical

---

[86] *Preparation for Death,* 319

[87] The famous story of the infestation of the Cranmer family home is recounted in the book, *The Demon of Brownsville Road,* by Bob Cramer and Erica Manfred. This infestation was connected with many evil deeds committed in the house in the past. The infestation and possession case in Gary, Indiana, in 2012, began with a curse on the family in the home.

presence.[88] Fr. Fortea also speaks about the ability of the demon to look at the priest "with an evil look" through the eyes of the possessed.[89]

Visiting cemeteries, haunted houses, and notoriously infested houses, as a form of entertainment, is a dangerous form of curiosity that opens the door to diabolical harassment. Haunted houses are real, but most people do not understand what they are dealing with and walk right in to a demon's activity.[90] It is possible that, instead of a demon, it is a departed soul who is present in the house. The two cases are very different in nature, effects, and purpose. The demon is evil, harmful, and makes life miserable inside the house. The human spirit is there solely to gain prayers and is not evil or harmful. Adam Blai says that, when the entity present is a demon, the minor exorcism prayers of the priest will have the effect of lifting an "evil pressure" from the dwelling and imparting a "noticeable lightness and clarity in the air."[91] Departed souls, on the other hand, "become completely still and silent" when a Mass is offered or prayers are said on their behalf.[92]

It is possible that the human spirit may initially be "spooky" only because its presence was unusual and unexpected. If it is a human spirit, all that needs to be done is to offer a Mass for the departed soul, and obtain a plenary indulgence on their behalf, and the person will depart.[93] The Vatican International Exhibition of Eucharistic miracles hands on a remarkable story to demonstrate this power of the Mass. In the town of Montserrat, in 1657, a young girl petitioned the Abbot Millán de Mirando to offer three Masses for her father whom she believed would then be freed from Purgatory. During the first Mass, her father appeared, surrounded by flames. To prove this vision, which only she could see, the priest asked the girl to place a tissue near the flames. When she did, it "began to burn with a lively flame." After

---

[88] Ripperger #1
[89] Fortea, 82
[90] Ripperger #1
[91] Blai, 48
[92] Blai, 38
[93] Ripperger #1

the third Mass, the girl witnessed her father, now clothed in white, ascend into the sky.[94]

Illness

Fr. Ripperger relates many incidents when demons can appear to cause all sorts of ailments, ranging from depression to physical illnesses. These illnesses are, essentially, not the same as the authentic kind. Many people are legitimately depressed, for reasons that emerge in the natural course of life. Many people are physically ill due to viruses, bacteria, or other bodily weaknesses. From his experience, most cases do not involve demonic activity. Nonetheless, demons can cause every form of illness and mental illness that would otherwise have a natural origin.[95]

What we know from Sacred Scripture and the teachings of St. Thomas supports what exorcists see in their work. When the angels came to punish Sodom, they were capable of striking with blindness the men who sought to attack them.[96] When St. Raphael came to Tobit in answer to his prayers, he was capable of removing the blindness that Tobit had endured. St. Thomas teaches that both the good and the bad angels "can exercise an *indirect* influence on human wills by stirring up images in the human imagination" and, by their natural powers, can "arouse sentient appetites and passions." They can also "work upon the human senses" either while in a visible form or "by disturbing the sense-functions themselves."[97] St. Thomas also says that angels can act upon men from within, in such a way that the "senses are changed in various ways."[98]

Regarding addiction, for example, demons can cause the feelings of a specific addiction, and can be the source of the craving that drives the person into addictive behavior. The only way to know if this is the case is by having a priest pray exorcism prayers over the person.[99] If the person responds to this prayer, then you know that a

---

[94] http://www.therealpresence.org/eucharst/mir/english_pdf/Montserrat.pdf
[95] Ripperger #1
[96] Genesis 19:11
[97] Glenn, 92
[98] Summa 1, Q. 114, A 4
[99] Ripperger #2

demon is involved. As Fr. Fortea says, "It is the prayer which will give us the assurance that one is dealing with a possession or not."[100] If the person does not respond, then it is likely an authentic addiction. The minor exorcism prayers are used first, and these typically have an effect. For those with an addiction or mental illness, if it is of diabolical origin, the symptoms will vanish completely for a time as a result of these prayers but will then return.[101]

Temptations

The ordinary way in which demons seek to influence man is through temptation. Everyone is subject to this sort of harassment, whereas the extraordinary ways are much less common. As Fr. Amorth says, "There are more victims of Satan's ordinary action than of his extraordinary action."[102] The devil prefers to act through ordinary temptations, where he can remain hidden and unnoticed and achieve greater gains in souls. When he works in the extraordinary ways, it reveals his presence, which can ultimately disturb his work.[103]

Fr. Ripperger notes that one approach demons will use is to dig up old memories and seek to use these against you.[104] It is not difficult to imagine what sorts of things they could dig up and the way in which they could use them. For those who are taking their spiritual lives seriously, this is a common experience. As was mentioned above, demons are also permitted to have access to our imagination, in addition to our memory. They can, for example, bring to your mind any pornographic image that you have ever seen, and use this to tempt you against chastity.[105] In addition to bringing up memories, demons can also attack your imagination with images that do not reside in your memory. A priest once told a story of a nun who, in Confession, mentioned having images in her head of a pornographic

---

[100] Fortea, 75
[101] Ripperger #2
[102] Amorth, 63
[103] Amorth, 68
[104] Ripperger #1
[105] Ripperger #6

nature. This nun had never seen anything of the sort, and the priest concluded that this was of diabolical origin.

Demons can also block your memories and your ability to remember certain things.[106] This prevents you from remembering the sin that was at the start of all your problems, and which is at the root of the more prominent sins with which you are currently struggling. If the demons can block your memory of that sin, they can also keep you from renouncing that sin, which would help break the hold it has on your life. Fr. Ripperger recommends that we ask Our Lady of Sorrows to reveal to us the true nature of the problem so we can effectively address it. This title of Our Lady is powerful for a reason and is addressed more in Chapter Ten.[107]

Demons also attack our perception of people and situations.[108] The most common form of this is to make evil appear good to us, to make us desire something, particularly at a weak moment, that we would never otherwise think was good for us. They can also twist how we understand what another person is trying to communicate to us. Since we are not able to directly convey our thoughts, intellect to intellect, like the angels, our words are vulnerable as they are transmitted from one person to another. Someone complimenting you might, for example, use a word or phrase that triggers a negative memory. This will then be used by the demons to make you think the other person's intentions are the complete opposite of what they actually are. We must also be careful how we speak, heeding the warning of St. Francis de Sales, who says, "Even if we do mean no harm, the Evil One means a great deal, and he will use those idle words as a sharp weapon against some neighbour's heart."[109]

This ability to influence our perception of things is one reason why the Church has always said that you must never rely on your emotions in the discernment of your spiritual life. Demons can both attack your emotions and imitate them within you, even, as Fr. Ripperger says, stirring up good feelings when you are considering evil, for example.[110] In making us feel certain emotions, they can give an

---

[106] Ripperger #6
[107] Page 149.
[108] Ripperger #6, #2
[109] *Introduction to the Devout Life*, 143
[110] Ripperger #6

emotional reward after we sin. Demons are extremely unhappy spiritual persons, and they seek to both make us miserable like they are and to mold us into their own image. The demons will seek to condition us to be animated by the same vices as they are, and thus begin to act in a manner that is in accord with their own behavior.[111]

Fr. Amorth says that, once the demons fell, they "radically changed their mission" in our regard. They are now focused, with their keen intellects, on the "unique objective of destroying men and making them their companions in misfortune."[112] St. Francis de Sales describes this misery of the demons as "sadness and melancholy" and that Satan uses sadness and depression to lead good men to give up the pursuit of doing good. He says, "The Evil One delights in sadness and melancholy, because they are his own characteristics. He will be in sadness and sorrow through all Eternity, and he would fain have all others the same."[113] It is by earnestly resisting the efforts of Satan to make us weary in doing good that we will be able to drive him away. As St. Paul says, "let us not grow weary in well-doing, for in due season we shall reap, if we do not lose heart."[114]

Attaching to Families

As was mentioned earlier, in spiritual warfare, we often have to deal with what is called a generational spirit. This is a demon who, as permitted by God, is particularly focused on attacking the members of a certain family line. Fr. Ripperger says that this demon enters through the authority structure that God permitted, and typically comes in through a sin committed by the father of the family. This complies with the literal wording of Exodus, in which the Lord says He will visit "the iniquity of the fathers upon the children to the third and the fourth generation."[115] This sin opens the door for the demon to enter the entire home.[116]

---

[111] Ripperger #8
[112] Amorth, 127
[113] *Devout Life*, 192
[114] Galatians 6:9
[115] Exodus 20:5
[116] Ripperger #1, #7

This sort of demon can travel within the family and down the family line through marriages. Often, when this is the case, a newly married spouse will notice a sudden change of a negative sort soon after the marriage occurs.[117] Removing generational spirits is one reason why there are exorcisms in the traditional rite of Baptism. These Baptismal exorcisms are also done to ensure the child is not burdened under any curse placed there as a means of revenge against the family.

The concept of a generational spirit may seem foreign to a lot of people. Fr. Thomas mentions that he, too, did not think it was a real thing until he entered into the work of an exorcist. For these cases, as he says, it is clear that the person affected had not done anything that would have led to the presence of the demon in their lives. The attestation in Sacred Scripture of this reality helps it become more believable, especially in light of the evidence. From what he has seen, it could be the result of involvement in the occult in the lives of one of the parents or grandparents. In order to remove it, it has proven helpful for the person to offer prayers of renunciation for whatever the sin was that was committed by the past generation.[118]

Demons seek to drive a wedge between the spouses, often simply through some of the temptations mentioned above. As Fr. Amorth says, "Today families are among the most targeted by the ordinary action of Satan, through the chilling of relationships as well as betrayals and divisions."[119] Fr. Ripperger highlights the importance of good communication between spouses as being effective in thwarting this attack. When spouses communicate, it sheds light on hidden interior issues that the demon knows about but that has remained unknown to the other spouse. By disclosing these personal feelings and thoughts to each other, the spouses thwart the attack of the demon and strengthen their own bond.[120] This communication is important due to the fact, as is evident in the universal decline of cultures, of the rise of attacks on children and the institution of matrimony, the intensity

---

[117] Ripperger #9
[118] Fr. Thomas #1
[119] Amorth, 89
[120] Ripperger #2

of which cannot be rightly understood without factoring in the operations of the diabolical.

Compendium I

+ Demons are real, personal, rational, spiritual beings who chose evil and set themselves in opposition to God and man.
+ Demons know that what they lost in Heaven we will one day gain by grace.
+ What exorcists see in their ministry is in harmony with what Sacred Scripture and the Church teach to be true.
+ Demons drive us to extremes and do everything they can to prevent us from thinking about God.
+ Demons seek to divide and attack and frustrate us.
+ Demons do whatever God will allow them to do. God does allow them to act, though within the limits that He sets.
+ The diabolical attack on mankind began with Eve – and pride is at the root of all of their sins.
+ When we sin, we essentially act like the demons and this opens doors to them.
+ We must stay away from things that are affiliated with the diabolical and not let curiosity lead us to test the spiritual realm.
+ Demons are permitted to influence our minds and our bodies and our external lives. Some of these influences are common, some are rare.
+ Demons prefer to work in hidden ways but will work extraordinarily to make us suffer more. When they manifest, it damages their plan, because it brings their existence into the light.
+ We must learn how to fight well and perseveringly against the demons.

Chapter Two

The Angelic Nature

As we consider this spiritual war in which we are all engaged, and the behaviors of the Evil One and his demons, a short consideration of the nature of these spirits will be enlightening. This present consideration of the angelic nature will not be exhaustive, as the Tradition of the Church has much to say on the matter, particularly in the writings of the Doctors of the Church.

The spirits that God first created, which we commonly refer to collectively as 'angels,' are pure spirits with an intellect and a will and are thus persons. Their intellect and their will are of an order far superior to that of human beings, who also have an intellect and a will and are persons. As we consider the nature of angels, it is important to recall that the demons are not protected and empowered in all of the same ways as the holy angels. This is due to the absence of sanctifying grace in the demons. One impact is seen in their ability to know things. As Msgr. Paul J. Glenn points out, "the fallen angels (or demons) are totally divorced from divine wisdom and hence, in things supernatural, there can be error or falsehood in their knowing."[1]

Angelic Knowledge

Angels are given infused knowledge, which is then naturally present in the angel, endowed in such a way by the Creator at the moment of its creation.[2] While we can also receive infused knowledge as a special grace from God, we acquire knowledge through the senses and through being taught by others and by God.

---

[1] Glenn, 51
[2] Summa 1, Q. 54, A 4

The infused knowledge of angels far surpasses the knowledge that we acquire. It includes a knowledge of all immaterial and material things. To the holy angels, God also imparts a knowledge of Himself, which is the beatific vision they enjoy as a result of their fidelity. Angels are incomparably more intelligent than men and possess a capacity to know more than we do.[3] As Msgr. Glenn describes, "The angelic mind is like a clear mirror that takes in the full meaning of what it turns upon."[4] While angels do not need to understand by reasoning, they are capable of doing so and of understanding the way that we think and reason.

Angels understand the plan of Divine Providence in as much as God permits them to understand.[5] Despite this incompleteness of their knowledge which, at the same time, contains no errors or falsehoods, they are very good at predicting what will happen. Their infused knowledge includes those things that happen after the moment of creation, in the created world, except for what happens in our interior lives. Thus, they know all that is happening throughout the world, as a gift from God. Given the great wealth of knowledge that they possess, the power of their intellects, their ability to move at the speed of thought, and the absence of any burden which would limit access to these powers, such as we experience through our weak flesh, angels are capable of factoring together more pieces of the puzzle, so to speak, than we could ever come close to doing. This could resemble an ability to 'see the future' but would not actually be seeing the true future, which is an ability only God naturally possesses.[6]

Angelic communication is also based in the intellect. While we speak with our vocal cords, through our bodies, angels do not have bodies, or any sort of physical form – they are pure spirits. Angels communicate by acting upon the intellect of another angel, with that angel's consent. As Fr. Ripperger describes, angelic communication, in modern terms, is a sort of telepathy.[7] Fr. Fortea says that if we direct our mind and will to a saint, or angel, or demon, they can hear us.

---

[3] Summa 1, Q. 54-57
[4] Glenn, 51
[5] Summa 1, Q. 58
[6] Summa 1, Q. 57, A 3-5
[7] Ripperger #5

He has seen this reality in an exorcism when the demon obeyed an order that he gave only mentally.[8]

St. Thomas says that "for one angel to speak to another angel means nothing else but that by his own will he directs his mental concept in such a way that it becomes known to the other."[9] Angels act upon us in similar ways, suggesting thoughts to us, to which we may consent or which we may reject. Consider what the experience of a typical diabolical temptation is like: a thought comes to us which is evil, we recognize it as evil, we reject it or consent to it and, if the latter, we embrace the thought as our own. The holy angels function in the same manner, but with ideas that are good and holy. Typically, it is very difficult to distinguish our own ideas from those coming from an angel or a demon.

Location

Angels do not occupy a place; they are 'here' or 'there' because they are exercising their power in that place and not in another.[10] A 'place' is only for a physical thing, which has to occupy a physical space because it takes up space. Consider yourself, or a tree, or a bird: physical things need a place to be. Angels are pure spirits, and possess no matter, and therefore do not need, nor take up, space, and are thus not occupying a place. However, they are active in this world, and that activity makes them 'here' or 'there.' They act on something by fixing their thoughts on something and can change their activity simply by changing their thoughts.[11]

Time

As they are not in a place, nor are they in time. There are three states of being in relation to time. There are those who were created in time and are living in time, such as men. We were created within this passing world and live in this passing world. For the angels, the term 'aeveternity' is used. They were created outside of time but are

---

[8] Fortea, 34
[9] Summa 1, Q. 107, A 2
[10] Summa 1, Q. 52
[11] Summa 1, Q. 52

capable of acting inside time and have an infused knowledge of what happens inside time. For God, we use the term 'aeternum.' God has no beginning and no end and is the Creator of time itself.[12]

Their Beginning

Angels were created in a state of sanctifying grace and infused with the theological virtues. However, they were not created in a state of glory in the sense of possessing the beatific vision. In their first moments, there were multiple instants which determined whether they would proceed to beatification or be damned.[13] As Fr. Ripperger explains, the first instant was an immediate perception of their assigned task, which had some sort of relation to Christ. God said to all the angels, "This is your assigned task, and this is how it relates to Christ." The angelic intellect is such that, as soon as they consider a thing, they immediately possess a complete understanding of that thing.[14]

The second instant was the immediate decision of whether to accept or reject the task assigned to them, which was the one act of charity required to achieve beatitude. As their knowledge of this task was full and complete, they fully understood the consequences of saying 'yes' or 'no.' Fr. Ripperger says that Satan gave his infamous "Non serviam!" because of the Incarnation and the fact that he would need to serve Our Lord in the flesh. Satan could also not accept the fact that 'the Woman' would be greater and more knowledgeable than all the other created beings, including himself. The prophecy in Genesis, "she shall crush your head,"[15] is the result of his rejection.[16]

St. Thomas quotes Origen to help us understand the curse issued against Satan after he tempted man to fall from grace as he did, "The serpent of old," he says, "did not from the first walk upon breast and

---

[12] Ripperger #5
[13] Summa 1, Q. 62
[14] Ripperger #5
[15] A famous translation from St. Jerome of Genesis 3:15 uses 'ipsa' instead of 'ipse' and thus presents 'she' instead of 'he' as the one who will crush the head of the serpent. It is an ancient tradition and one which is settled within Sacred Tradition.
[16] Ripperger #5. This is one of many theories regarding the Fall of the angels.

belly."[17]   As St. Thomas states, this demonstrates that the devil was created good and it was only after his rejection of God's will for him that he lost grace and was damned.

Contrarily, the first thought of our Guardian Angels was that they were assigned to us to protect us.   They immediately said 'yes' and then merited the grace of glory and beheld God face to face.   As soon as we were created, they began their undaunted task of protecting us and fighting for our salvation.   All the while, as they look upon us, they continuously behold God in all His glory.   As a result of this beatification, "the beatified angel can neither will nor act, except as aiming towards God.   Now whoever wills or acts in this manner cannot sin."[18]

The third instant was the permanent fixing of their wills in this fundamental choice.   Their wills were confirmed in either good or evil, and they were either immediately damned or immediately saw God face to face.   God has mercy on man and not the angels because we are far less intelligent and do not fully understand what we are doing.   Angels, on the contrary, as they possess far superior intellects and wills, fully understand the consequences of their actions.

---

[17] Summa 1, Q. 63, A 6
[18] Summa 1, Q. 62, A 8

Compendium II

+ Demons are fallen angels. They possess the same kind of nature as the holy angels, but with limitations.
+ The power of the demons is limited in part due to the absence of sanctifying grace, which also limits their understanding of God's plan and leads them to make mistakes.
+ The angelic intellect is very keen and perceptive of all things and is given immense infused knowledge by God.
+ Though they cannot see the future, their vast knowledge and intellectual powers gives them an impressive ability to perceive and predict the course that the future will take. Neither the angels nor the demons can actually see the future.
+ Angels communicate by acting on the intellect of another angel. They can act on our intellects in the same way.
+ Angels are said to be in a place based on their activity in that place.
+ Angels merited beatification at the first moment after they were created, when they chose to obey God's will and serve Him. This is the same moment when the demons chose to disobey.
+ The first thought of our Guardian Angels was that they wanted to serve God by protecting us.
+ Once the angels made their choice, their wills became fixed in this decision, because they had perfect clarity regarding their choice.

Chapter Three

The Stages of Diabolical Influence

Diabolical influence appears in six forms with regard to human beings and in one with regard to animals and other material things. The six forms are: temptation, vexation, oppression, obsession, possession, and subjugation. The form related to animals, and other material things, is referred to as infestation.[1]

Ordinary Diabolical Influence – Temptation

The typical, constant, and recurring form of diabolical influence, to which each and every man will always be subject, involves the various forms of temptation by which the demons seek to erode our faith, hope, and charity and steal us away from a state of grace. These temptations are typically subtle but are always crafty and coordinated with the above-mentioned goal expressly in the mind of the demon. This subtlety is reflected in how Fr. Fortea describes temptation. He says, "Demons tempt us by infusing thoughts into our minds. In other words, a demon introduces into our reason, memory, and imagination intellectual objects proper to our understanding that cannot be distinguished from our own thoughts."[2] One of the keys here is that the temptation "cannot be distinguished" from what we perceive to be our own thinking about an idea. If we cannot make that distinction, we are much more likely to follow the temptation. Careful discernment of our thoughts can often unmask the devil's work.

The initial temptation with Eve is an example of this form of influence. When Eve listened to the serpent, she allowed him to

---

[1] See page 15 and following.
[2] Fortea, 47

interact with her mind and imagination. The ideas he proposed to her stirred her emotions and, filled with a deceitful twist of the words imparted to her by God Himself, they appeared to her as something delightful and worthy of her consent. They also stirred her self-centeredness, which is pride, and the root of every fall, including that of Satan himself.

St. Francis de Sales recounts a violent assault on the imagination of St. Catherine of Siena, which demonstrates what God permits and what Satan is capable of doing. He states,

> "The Evil One having obtained permission from God to assault that pious virgin with all his strength, so long as he laid no hand upon her, filled her heart with impure suggestions, and surrounded her with every conceivable temptation of sight and sound, which, penetrating into the Saint's heart, so filled it, that, as she herself has said, nothing remained free save her most acute superior will."[3]

If this craftiness was likewise applied in the attack on Eve, it is not surprising that she fell.

Extraordinary Diabolical Influence

The next five examples are called extraordinary diabolical influences. These are rare and above and beyond the normal temptations which are experienced by every human person on a daily basis. These do not occur as often as temptations, though as exorcists see they are becoming more common today.

Vexation

The modern term to refer to this category of diabolical influence is vexation. This is when demons are given permission by God to physically abuse a person. Typically, the people permitted to be attacked in this way are the saints, though not exclusively. It can sometimes manifest in cases of severe infestation of a home, for ex-

---

[3] *Devout Life*, 182

ample.[4] This is very rare and the reason God allows it to occur is to bring about the further sanctification of the person and the humiliation of the demon.[5] Though it is typically an experience which only the saints go through, today, with the increase in grave sins and superstition and people living in a state of sin, these experiences are becoming more common.

This category includes injuries that are caused by inexplicable events, such as scrapes or cuts on the body without any explanation,[6] as well as pulling hair and pushing people down stairs. In the lives of the saints, we can read about physical assaults, as with fists (St. Pio of Pietrelcina), and setting furniture on fire (St. John Vianney). St Teresa of Avila suffered similar assaults from demons. After one such attack, after dispelling them with holy water, some of her sisters entered her room and smelled a foul odor, like brimstone.[7] As Fr. Jeffrey Grob has noted, oppression, in its attack on the senses, can also lead to a situation where "everything a person smells or tastes is putrid."[8]

According to Fr. Amorth, vexation can also take the form of nightmares in which the person dreams of acting in evil ways. This form of vexation is similar to diabolical obsession.[9] Adam Blai lists demonic nightmares under potential signs (secondary) of a case of home infestation of an evil spirit. As he says, these are not always an indicator, as nightmares are common for people and typically indicative of processing stress. Diabolical nightmares are, as he calls them, "persistent, repetitive, and out of character for the person."[10] To be a case of infestation, more dramatic signs would also be present.

Oppression

Diabolical oppression involves those things that affect a person's life from the outside. These can include all aspects of a person's life.

---

[4] *Demon of Brownsville Road* and the case in Gary, Indiana.
[5] Ripperger #2
[6] Fr. Grob article
[7] *Life of Teresa*, 174
[8] Fr. Grob article
[9] Amorth, 71
[10] Blai, 42

From their experiences, exorcists have witnessed these extraordinary manifestations firsthand. Fr. Ripperger says that diabolical oppression can appear as inexplicable financial difficulties, such as the inability to obtain employment despite being highly qualified and applying for multiple jobs, or being fired all of a sudden. Oppression can manifest and cause a person's possessions to chronically break down, despite reasonable efforts to keep them in good order.[11] Fr. Amorth points out that it can also cause divisions within marriages, tear apart friendships, and leave the person isolated.[12] This is, of course, the goal of the devil who, as Fr. Grob mentions, "lives to instill fear and isolation in the human soul."[13]

Everyday life, such as in jobs, can be affected by oppression as well. Fr. Ripperger said he was helping a doctor for whom many patients were refusing to pay and were simply not showing up for appointments. He wrote a prayer for him to address the matter and the problem resolved within a week.[14]

This author, after studying Fr. Ripperger's teachings, and discerning prudent responses to similar peculiar situations, had a friend in a similar situation as this doctor. For years, this friend had the experience of seeing clients with the most peculiar and atypically complicated situations. Other professionals, with whom they worked, agreed that something was odd and that a "black cloud" seemed to be following them. The experience was the same at multiple offices where they had worked. I wrote a prayer that addressed the specific problem that seemed to be at the root of all of this, using the general spiritual warfare wisdom that Father teaches, and gave the prayer to this friend. Just as Father describes, the prayer worked as if it was blocking something. On the days when this friend forgets to say the prayer, the experience in the office is as bizarre as it used to be.

Oppression can affect relationships in a number of ways. A woman whom Fr. Ripperger was assisting, was suffering under the Freemasonic curse, from which he helped her break free. Before that moment, the woman had been estranged from her five daughters for

[11] Ripperger #1, #2
[12] Amorth, 72
[13] Fr. Grob article
[14] Ripperger #2

The Stages of Diabolical Influence

According to Fr. Ripperger, diabolic obsession can come and go and not be persistent. It starts quickly and can end quickly, bringing strong emotions which are not based in reality. The person can become extraordinarily angry for no reason, or depressed to a high degree, and then it can lift suddenly and stop. He says that Our Lord does not allow a constant obsession but one which comes and goes with highs and lows. If the situation is not properly addressed, the obsession can become more intense.[26]

There is a real psychological illness, bipolar, which resembles diabolic obsession, and it is important to distinguish this from obsession. Often, as Fr. Ripperger says, bipolar ends up being diabolic obsession, or having a diabolical component. Father says that he has had wonderful success praying the old rite exorcism over people with bipolar.[27] Sometimes, after repeated sessions of prayer, the symptoms would gradually disappear for longer lengths of time and enable people to get off of their medications. Recourse to Confession brings similar results for those suffering from diabolical influence. After confessing, the temptations will subside but later reappear. When the problem is psychological only, Confession does not have the same impact.[28]

The best way to combat diabolical obsession is humility and mental prayer. Humility is the most powerful thing to protect yourself. St. Louis de Montfort says that the humble servants of Mary, in union with her, will crush the head of Satan with their humility.[29] St. Louis de Montfort has a powerful statement on humility, worth quoting in full in the present context:

> "The evil spirits, cunning thieves that they are, can take us by surprise and rob us of all we possess. They are watching day and night for the right moment. They roam incessantly seeking to devour us and to snatch from us in one brief moment of sin all the grace and merit we have taken years to acquire. Their malice and their experience, their cunning and their numbers ought to make us ever fearful of such a misfortune

---

[26] Ripperger #2
[27] The Rite of Exorcism was changed in 1999.
[28] Ripperger #2
[29] *True Devotion*, 54

happening to us. People, richer in grace and virtue, more experienced and advanced in holiness than we are, have been caught off their guard and robbed and stripped of everything. How many cedars of Lebanon, how many stars of the firmament have we sadly watched fall and lose in a short time their loftiness and their brightness! What has brought about this unexpected reverse? Not the lack of grace, for this is denied no one. It was a lack of humility; they considered themselves stronger and more self-sufficient than they really were. They thought themselves well able to hold on to their treasures. They believed their house secure enough and their coffers strong enough to safeguard their precious treasure of grace. It was because of their unconscious reliance on self – although it seemed to them that they were relying solely on the grace of God – that the most just Lord left them to themselves and allowed them to be despoiled."[30]

Since pride is a corruption of the way we think, practicing custody of the mind is of great benefit for controlling our thoughts and becoming more alert to the start of temptations. Before the obsession has time to settle into your mind, mental prayer[31] and meditation can break the obsession and prevent it from becoming rooted and problematic. As St. Alphonsus says, "Meditation is the blessed furnace in which divine love is lighted up."[32] He adds, "God enlightens us in meditation. In meditation God speaks to us and makes known to us what we are to avoid, and what we are to do."[33] Deliverance prayers[34] are also helpful in dealing with obsession.

Possession

More severe than all the other forms of diabolical influence which have been previously mentioned, possession is when a demon takes over either one part (partial) or the entire body (full) of a person.

---

[30] *True Devotion*, 88
[31] See footnote on pg 129.
[32] St. Alphonsus equates mental prayer with meditation.
[33] *Preparation*, 323
[34] By priests, or by oneself with a properly approved prayer.

Typically, possession is only partial. Full possession is the gravest form and makes the entire body subject to the demon. The cases of diabolical possession are rare. There are many more cases of vexation, obsession, and infestation.[35] However, like the lesser forms of diabolical influence, possession is becoming more common now. Fr. Ripperger states that approximately three out of every one hundred and fifty cases which he investigates ends up being a case of possession. Fr. Grob estimates that about eighty-five percent of people who come to him do not need an exorcist. Some still need a priest, but others would only benefit from a counselor.[36]

There are three ways that a person might become possessed. It is not always the result of an evil deed on the person's part. A person can become possessed through mortal sin,[37] which is the most common. As Fr. Fortea says, people can become possessed by "making a pact with the devil, taking part in spiritualist sessions, satanic cults, or esoteric rites, offering one's child to Satan, being the victim of witchcraft." "Possession," he adds, "is not contagious," a door must be opened.[38] The mortal sins that lead to possession are not necessarily extreme sins, but include pride and fornication, not just murder.

People can also become possessed as a result of something gravely evil happening to the person, and where the proper healing is not achieved. This can send the person in a downward spiral, trapped in a world of negative emotions.[39] Finally, possession can also come about simply by the will of God, which, of course, is much rarer than any other manifestation of the demonic.[40]

Some people who are possessed are able to hold down jobs and carry on a normal life, without anyone knowing they are possessed.[41] The demon will only manifest once in a while.[42] For others, it may be the case that they cannot function at all and are unable to pray. The

---

[35] Amorth, 66

[36] Fr. Grob video

[37] Mortal sin leads to spiritual death. After committing a mortal sin, and before confessing that sin, a man is in a "state of mortal sin." This is a state without the protection of God's grace and, thus, vulnerable to the internal and external activity of Satan.

[38] Fortea, 82

[39] Fr. Grob video

[40] These will be explored in more detail in Chapter Nine.

[41] Amorth, 82

[42] Ripperger #2

symptoms of possession can alternate between possession and normal living. Sometimes the possession will manifest when provoked by external events, like stress or an experience of the sacred, such as in the exorcism rite.[43]

When the demon manifests, the person has no control over what they are doing. Some people essentially black out and have no idea what is happening. Demons can also suppress the faculties in the body so much that it is as if the person is simply watching the demon use their body.[44] The possessed may be subject to interior assaults of the devil, including trembling legs, headaches, and other pains and illnesses. In the more serious cases – the person is unable to have a stable life. Each case is different. Some are able to pray and go to Mass, while others are not.[45]

Liberating a person from a full possession is difficult since, in this case, the person has given their will over to the demon. The first thing the exorcist must do is ask the person if they want to be liberated.[46] As shocking as it may sound, there are some possessed people who do not wish to be liberated. In the case of possession, as Fr. Ripperger describes it, the demon establishes an abusive relationship with the possessed. It may start as a peaceful slavery relationship but, once the person resists the demon, the relationship becomes abusive.[47]

The temptation from a demon proceeds from a careful analysis in order to successfully achieve a desired outcome.[48] Their decision to enter a person when the door is open is not necessarily well thought out, though. Though they do have free will, demons do not possess virtue, which would stop them from giving in to the temptation to possess someone, especially when they should be able to see that it will end up causing themselves a great deal of suffering. Instead, enslaved by their wills, fixed on evil, the demons are impulsive and seek the immediate gratification from the harm they can inflict.[49]

---

[43] Amorth, 67
[44] Ripperger #3
[45] Amorth, 82
[46] Ripperger #1
[47] Ripperger #1
[48] Fortea, 50
[49] Fortea, 84

When they are tempting the person and attempting to gain entry, they look for certain physiological signs that reveal that the person has given consent. Demons cannot know the person's will specifically, as this is not in the powers of the angelic nature. They are able to read bodily reactions which come with the person's thoughts and which show that the person has consented. As Fr. Ripperger points out, modern science has confirmed that there are bodily signs that accompany a person's thoughts, such as when the person is lying. Demons know to look for these in order to determine the person's thoughts.[50] As Fr. Amorth says, a demon cannot read our thoughts, "he can only surmise it through observing our behavior. It is not a complicated operation for him, having an extremely fine intelligence." A demon can decide how to tempt us by observing "what we read, see, say, and experience, and from the companions we choose, even from our glances – from all this he can discern where he will tempt us and at which particular moment. And that is what he does."[51]

Subjugation

The last form of diabolical influence is called subjugation. As Fr. Ripperger says, this involves literally making a pact with the devil or a demon and submitting oneself to his lordship.[52] It is an agreement with the devil based on something that the devil has offered. The concept of making a pact with the devil occurs as early as the fifth century, as recorded by St. Jerome. Making a pact with the devil does not always bring what is desired, as exorcists have witnessed. The devil is a liar, not a benefactor.[53] Satan cannot truly enter into a contract of this sort, because he cannot guarantee that he will give what he has promised. Everything that the devil does is what God permits him to do, and he cannot do anything unless God permits it. That being said, sometimes these pacts do produce what they promise.[54]

According to Fr. Amorth, when one becomes a Satanist, typically the experience, in the beginning, is that all of the promises "come eas-

---

[50] Ripperger #3
[51] Amorth, 20
[52] Ripperger #3
[53] Fortea, 29
[54] Ripperger #2

ily and [it] seems to be a great and beautiful affair." Before long, though, it becomes clear that Satan has "taken them for a ride" and their life becomes one of intense suffering. In the lives of people he has helped, Fr. Amorth has witnessed Satan fulfilling his promises of success and riches, only to then quickly demand the soul of the person involved, leading them into moments of intense hatred toward others which they could hardly resist.[55]

Regardless of the defect of such a contract, they still happen. According to Fr. Ripperger, these pacts are more common than people think, especially in Hollywood, where it is a big problem.[56] Many of these are quite publicly known. John Lennon, for example, is reported to have made a pact with the devil before he and the Beatles became famous. The pact involved a period of twenty years. Almost twenty years to the day of the pact, John Lennon was shot.[57] This form of diabolical influence is usually the hardest to break. There are many factors which make these pacts so strong. As Fr. Fortea says, "The great destructive power of a pact is that the person may think he is condemned no matter what he does."[58] If the person can be reached with the hope of grace, it would then, of course, be possible to overcome the contract and the diabolical effects it has brought.

There are some people, though, who choose evil and desire to remain with the evil. Fr. Amorth had a young man brought to him by his mother and sister. The man smoked, cursed, and used and sold drugs. When Fr. Amorth began to pray with him, the demon manifested violently and Fr. Amorth had to stop. After telling the man that he was possessed, the man stated that he was already aware of that fact and had no problem with it. Fr. Amorth never saw the man again.[59]

This choice to remain possessed can be connected to the original promise of companionship or power which the demon offered. The allure of power and the "camaraderie and approval to all the negative emotions" which the person has been experiencing can lead the per-

---

[55] Amorth, 34

[56] Ripperger #2

[57] Recounted in Lennon biographies, such as those by Ray Coleman, Albert Goldman, and Joseph Niezgoda, in addition to other documentaries about the Beatles.

[58] Fortea, 30

[59] Amorth, 76

son to permit the demon to enter more and more deeply into their life. The person may have willingly permitted the possession to occur as a result of this manner of approach. Eventually, the person may feel so attached to the demon that "they don't know who they are without the demon, even though its presence is terrifying."[60]

---

[60] Blai, 20f

Compendium III

+ Demons cleverly impart thoughts into our minds in ways that are nearly impossible to detect.
+ Sometimes the demons will attack the mind, overwhelming it with ideas and images, in order to break the will and move the person to sin.
+ All mankind is subject to ordinary temptation and must do battle daily to avoid sin.
+ Extraordinary diabolical activities are typically rare but are all becoming more common today.
+ To suffer from these, typically a door must be willingly opened to the diabolical, either by the individual or by another person against the individual.
+ In these extraordinary manifestations, demons are allowed to attack the imagination of the person, the senses of the person, the person's possessions, and at times the body of the person.
+ Demons are also allowed to orchestrate external events in a manner designed to inflict harm or suffering upon the person or bring aggravations into the person's life.
+ Demons are also allowed to cause apparent illnesses. These will merely be symptoms resembling a real illness but will only be driven away by prayers.
+ Humility, mental prayer and meditation, and recourse to our Guardian Angels are means to protect us against diabolical obsession.
+ Demons observe and study us but cannot see our thoughts. They build their attack around our weaknesses and wounds.
+ Some people choose to make pacts with the devil. While the devil is a liar, he often still gives what was promised, but completely destroys the person's life in the process, in a strategic way designed to lead them to damnation.

Chapter Four

The Authority of Our Lord over Demons

As is obvious from the teachings of our Holy Catholic Faith, God is the Supreme over all things. He is the sole Creator and all that exists owes its existence to Him. Further, no creature is capable of operating outside of what God has permitted for it in its nature. Creatures with free will are capable of acting against their own nature, but only in a manner that destroys it, not in a manner that elevates it. Only God, through the gift of grace, is able to elevate the nature of a creature to a higher state. Here, we will look at some of the ways in which God, while permitting the rebellious activity of the demons, blocks them from acting beyond what He has permitted them to do.

Contrary to what might come to mind for many, demons, though they are in a state of rebellion against God, are not completely independent of Him. That was one of the things that Satan desired: to have, as St. Thomas described it, "final beatitude of his own power, whereas this is proper to God alone."[1] This was not possible for him, since he was and will always remain a mere creature, necessarily dependent on God. Though they may rebel, the demons can have no complete and successful mutiny, for God is, by nature, the sole Omnipotent.

As a result, Satan and the demons are completely under Our Lord's control. Everything they do is, therefore, what is permitted by Him, even though all of these rebellious acts are contrary to His desire for them. The actions of the demons fall under the permissive will of the Lord. God permits what is beneficial for us spiritually and what can be used by us advantageously. Thus, even the activity of the demons can be used to our benefit. As Fr. Ripperger says, demons are

---

[1] Summa 1, Q. 63, A 3

on a short leash; Christ is in absolute control over everything in the spiritual realm, and the demons know this.[2]

Recall the scene when Our Lord sends the demons into the pigs.[3] Within the man was "Legion," meaning there were a great many demons and, when the man first saw Jesus, the demons cried out and requested that Jesus not torment them. Then, they asked that He not send them down to Hell but petitioned that they be allowed to enter into the herd of swine. Our Lord then allowed it, and they immediately departed from the man, entered the swine, and ran them headlong over the cliff. This is a clear example of how the demons know that Christ has the only say in these matters. Even though they rebel against Him in every way possible, when He appears before them, they fall to their faces, grovel, beg, and obey.

In St. Thomas' commentary on the Gospel of Matthew,[4] he discusses Our Lord's reaction to the final temptation which Satan brought against Him. In this scene, we can see how Our Lord Himself endured the temptations of the devil, but only to a point. St. Thomas says, "Note that Christ had heard many insults, but did not care. But this, *if you will fall down and adore me*, he did not endure, because the others were insults against himself, but this one was an insult against God." St. Thomas says that the first two insults were against Christ in His human nature, but the last one, seeking His adoration, offended God directly. St. Thomas continues, saying, "Therefore, he says *Be gone, Satan!*...Note also that it is not in the devil's power to tempt as much as he wills, but as much as God permits; hence, he says *Be gone!*" St. Thomas then quotes, in this context, what the Lord says to Job, regarding His creation of the sea, here applying it to the demons: "Thus far shall you come and no farther, and here shall your proud waves be stayed."[5]

Even though demons are on a short leash, God does not stop them from entering into our lives, either for our spiritual betterment or as a punishment. Our Lord determines what the demon can and cannot do once the person invites the demon in, or if the demon arrives

---

[2] Ripperger #6
[3] Luke 8:26-39
[4] St. Thomas, Commentary, Gospel of Matthew 4
[5] Job 38:11

on his own. St. Teresa of Avila, who was often assaulted by the demons, was greatly comforted, despite the ongoing attacks, when she realized how limited the demons were in their power against her. She remarked, "So often have these accursed creatures tormented me and so little am I afraid of them, now that I see they cannot stir unless the Lord allows them to."[6]

In one exorcism, Fr. Ripperger saw a woman who was possessed only in her lower back.[7] As he extracted information from the demon, the demon admitted that he did not know why he was possessing only that part. All the demon admitted to knowing was that Christ had restricted him to that part of the body when he had entered the woman. Also, regarding diabolical obsession, Fr. Ripperger says that Our Lord does not allow a constant obsession. The demon is only permitted to obsess the mind for a period of time before granting the person a reprieve. The obsession will then return later, especially if the person does not seek to resolve the problem.[8]

Our Lord also wields His authority over the demons through the use of what Fr. Ripperger referred to as a "nemesis." When the exorcist gains the name of the demon who is the possessor, he can then invoke the assistance of the demon's nemesis. The nemesis can be Our Lord or Our Lady under a specific title or one of the saints. Fr. Amorth says that the demons often refer to Our Lady as the "thief of souls" and the saints are called "assassins." Demons will not pronounce the names of Jesus, Mary, and the saints during an exorcism, unless when under duress and compelled to do so.[9] Fr. Ripperger says that every demon has a nemesis: to Lucifer, it is Christ; to Satan, it is the Father; to Beelzebub, it is the Immaculate Heart. Another example is Saint Catherine of Sienna. She is the nemesis to the "noonday devil," who admitted this during an exorcism owing to the fact that she conquered him in her earthly life.[10] The noonday devil comes from Psalm 91, and is understood to be the demon of acedia, or spiritual sloth and laziness.

---

[6] *Life of Teresa*, 175
[7] Ripperger #6
[8] Ripperger #2
[9] Amorth, 127
[10] Ripperger #1, #7

Fr. Piero Catalano, a pupil of Fr. Amorth, says that he invokes the assistance of Padre Pio in the exorcisms he performs. When Padre Pio begins to assist, Fr. Catalano says, "The possessed person becomes afraid. He'll say, 'The one with the beard is here!' And I reply, 'By any chance, is he named Saint Pio of Pietrelcina?' The demon will respond, 'No, his name is Francesco Forgione.' The devil fears even to name him."[11] Fr. Amorth spoke of a similar success invoking the assistance of Pope John Paul II. As he says, "When I pronounce his name, the demons are literally infuriated."[12]

Fr. Carlos Martins told a fascinating story about an exorcist friend of his, with the pseudonym "Fr. George," who, during an exorcism, was told by the demon that his nemesis was St. Thomas Beckett. Fr. George then spoke to Fr. Martins the very next day and told him about the demon's nemesis. Fr. Martins runs "Treasures of the Church," a renowned organization that travels the world and presents about one hundred and fifty relics of many great saints for the faithful to venerate. Fr. Martins immediately sent a first-class relic of St. Thomas Beckett to the exorcist, who used it in the exorcism. Fr. Martins says that, when the exorcist applied the relic, "the effect was as if all hell broke loose. The demon screamed horribly, as if he was being tortured. In fact, the reaction was so much, that it took Fr. George aback. Under that torture, the demon subsequently revealed that he was the demon who had possessed the king's men that had murdered Thomas à Beckett."[13]

The protection that priests receive with the help of these nemeses, and the other protections that Our Lord provides, is very comforting to exorcists. Two examples will demonstrate why. Fr. Catalano revealed that in one exorcism, the demon sought to tempt him away from his ministry with an offer of worldly riches. When Father declined, the demon responded, "If I could, I'd kill you instantly."[14] Fr. Ripperger had a very similar encounter when exorcising the noonday devil mentioned above. During the exorcism, the demon stopped and

---

[11] Fr. Piero Catalano article, by Gelsomino Del Guercio for Aleteia.org, from an interview originally published by the *Corriere Della Sera*, Dec. 2017, by Antonio Crispino.
[12] Amorth, 126
[13] http://www.courageouspriest.com/warning-attempt-exorcism-home
[14] Fr. Piero Catalano article

said to him, "If you weren't being protected, I'd snap your neck."[15] This goes back to what Fr. Fortea said about the demons' inability to love: "The capacity to love has been annihilated in the psychology of a demon."[16] All that is left, as is seen in the work of exorcists, is a brutal hatred. Of course, as we have also seen, the demons cannot touch us unless God permits it, and He typically does not.

Unfortunately, as Fr. Thomas tells us, God occasionally, though very rarely, allows a priest to be injured during an exorcism. When he was helping to train a new exorcist, the possessed person, who was being held down by five strong men, was able to "bolt out of the grasp of those men" and attack the priest who was watching the exorcism. The priest was unfortunately injured to some extent.[17] Hopefully, this was a sign that the priest was especially favored by God for this ministry and the demon was furious as a result.

After a successful exorcism, when the demon has been cast out, it is up to Our Lord, and not the exorcist, as to where the demon is sent. Fr. Ripperger says that demons hate to admit that everyone, even the demon himself, is a slave to Christ and subject to His command. Nonetheless, Our Lord decides where they go.[18] In addition to the example of Legion, Our Lord clearly states[19] that, after being cast out of a person, demons roam around the earth, restless, and often return to the person whom they had previously possessed.[20] Further, He states, they bring stronger demons with them upon their return.

Fr. Ripperger says it is the job of the exorcist to make the process of expelling the demon so painful for them that they would rather be in Hell than possess someone again.[21] He often uses the term "beatings" to describe what the demon is experiencing in the process. Fr. Fortea uses the term "torture" to refer to what the demon endures in the exorcism.[22] Fr. Thomas also speaks of the power of the ritual of

---

[15] Ripperger #6

[16] Fortea, 18

[17] Fr. Thomas #2

[18] Ripperger #1

[19] Matthew 12:43ff

[20] see page 112 for a brief story about a woman whom Father observed to achieve a high degree of holiness as a result of her struggle with possession. See also Chapter 10 on how to protect your spiritual life against diabolical activity.

[21] Ripperger #1

[22] Fortea, 109

exorcism to inflict pain on the demons. He says, "I've seen, when you're praying those prayers, and you mean them, they do incredible harm and pain to those demons."[23]

Though the demons seek to devour all of us when they find us in sin or successfully coax us to fall, God blocks them from proceeding with possession, even though, as Fr. Ripperger says, this is the proper effect of mortal sin.[24] Thus, God's mercy toward man overpowers the natural abilities of the demons, in most cases. Fr. Ripperger describes how rational creatures stand in one of the fivefold relationships with God's mercy: Angels are not in need of God's mercy; demons make no claim to God's mercy, and have cut themselves off from it; the damned in Hell had it at one point but rejected it; saints in Heaven have it completely; and men on earth are at least partially receiving it at all times because God is blocking the full effects of sin and the powers of the demonic.[25] Every time we commit a mortal sin, we merit damnation, but God offers mercy first. Every time we commit a mortal sin, the door is open to the demons possessing us, but God blocks them in most cases.

In the Name of Jesus

A final point. Throughout history, in all cultures, as Fr. Amorth says, there has existed some form of awareness of diabolical possession. The ancient rituals that were used to protect people from malevolent forces can be seen as "precursors of the prayer of exorcism not yet illuminated by the truth of Christ." As we can see in the Gospels, the Jews also practiced exorcism rituals. When Our Lord began His public ministry though, He did not rely on the rituals of the Jews, but "drove out demons based solely on the power of His Word."[26] When returning to Our Lord after having been sent out, the Apostles remarked with joy, "Lord, even the demons are subject to us in your name!"[27]

---

[23] Fr. Thomas #2
[24] Ripperger #1
[25] Ripperger #3
[26] Amorth, 97
[27] Luke 10:17

The Authority of Our Lord over Demons

In spiritual warfare, we invoke the Name of Jesus to gain authority over the demons that are harassing us, and to repel and disperse them. This is a central and powerful element of the rite of exorcism as well. The power of this Holy Name of Jesus is wonderfully attested to in Sacred Scripture: by the invocation of the Holy Name of Jesus, sins are forgiven,[28] healings are performed,[29] the Truth is proclaimed,[30] demons are cast out,[31] divisions are rejected,[32] sin is condemned,[33] and the power and authority of Our Lord is made manifest.[34]

We also invoke the names of all those things which are sanctified by their deep relationship with Our Lord. Thus, Our Lady and the saints are invoked, for they conquered the devil and the devil has not forgotten the shame he experienced in losing those battles. Plus, these saints, who have merited to be seated in glory among the Angels in Heaven, have gained, through their victory, a certain authority over evil and authority in the work of salvation. The demons now fear them, for they know and see that God is working through them. Fr. Ripperger says that demons know whether someone is in Heaven or in Purgatory. One saint said that God occasionally pulls back the separation between Hell and Heaven, allowing the damned and the demons to see the Blessed enjoying God. They can see the enjoyment the Blessed experience, but they cannot see God Himself.[35]

We also invoke those things which are the primary means of Our Lord's victory over evil. Thus, His Name is invoked, for that refers to His Person. The Holy Cross is invoked, for that is the sign of His victory over evil. A further and most powerful invocation is that of the Most Precious Blood of Jesus. The Precious Blood is important for one central reason: it is that Blood which was sacrificially shed by the same Jesus whose Name is all-powerful; which was shed in order to ransom us from captivity to the devil and sanctify us with His own divine life. The invocation of the Most Precious Blood of Jesus sol-

---

[28] Acts 2:38
[29] Acts 3:6
[30] Acts 4:18
[31] Acts 16:18
[32] I Cor. 1:10
[33] I Cor. 5:4
[34] Philippians 2:9-11
[35] Ripperger #1

emnly declares and imparts the defeat of the power of Satan over souls.

Our Lord is truly sovereign over the spiritual battle in which we find ourselves. He does not abandon us when He permits the work of evil, for this permission is only oriented toward achieving a greater good. Further, He does not permit the work of evil to operate with a power that exceeds our own strength, so long as we abide in Him.

A Hymn in honor of the Most Precious Blood of Jesus[36]

Glory be to Jesus!
Who in bitter pains
Pour'd for me the life-blood
From His sacred veins.

Grace and life eternal
In that Blood I find;
Bless'd be His compassion,
Infinitely kind!

Bless'd through endless ages
Be the precious stream,
Which from endless torment
Doth the world redeem.

There the fainting spirit
Drinks of life her fill;
There, as in a fountain,
Laves herself at will.

O the Blood of Christ!
It soothes the Father's ire;
Open the gate of heaven,
Quells eternal fire.

---

[36] From the *Raccolta* #37

The Authority of Our Lord over Demons

Abel's blood for vengeance
Pleaded to the skies;
But the Blood of Jesus
For our pardon cries.

Oft as it is sprinkled
On our guilty hearts,
Satan in confusion
Terror-struck departs.

Oft as earth exulting
Wafts its praise on high,
Hell with terror trembles,
Heaven is filled with joy.

Lift ye, then, your voices;
Swell the mighty flood;
Louder still and louder,
Praise the Precious Blood.

Compendium IV

+ Our Lord has complete control over the demons. They are only allowed to do what He permits them to do.
+ In most cases God blocks the demons from doing what they would prefer to do to us.
+ Sacred Scripture, the lives of the saints, and the work of exorcists demonstrate the reality of this limitation on diabolical activity.
+ The angels and the saints constantly work against the actions of the demons. Certain saints are pitted against certain demons to specifically block and oppose their evil efforts.
+ The work of the Communion of Saints is important because exorcists also see how much the demons hate us and them, often from the mouths of the demons themselves.
+ The exorcism inflicts a real pain upon the demon which, as a result, is effective in driving them out of a person's body.
+ The demons fear everything that points to God or has been sanctified by its union with Him, especially the Holy Name of Jesus and the invocation of the Most Precious Blood of Jesus.

Chapter Five

How Exorcists Know What They Know

When listening to an exorcist give a talk, most people, at some point, stop and ponder where the exorcist learned what he is telling us. Are there courses on demonology and exorcism in seminary? Are there manuals where the Church has recorded everything that exorcists have learned and that the Vatican distributes to priests throughout the world? While there are some courses and manuals, it isn't so simple to train an exorcist.

The art of exorcising demons is less a clearly and completely revealed dimension of Catholic theology as it is an accumulation of information resulting from interactions with the demonic by priests who possess the authority to command them. There are many teachings which inform priests and provide them with a foundation of knowledge as they begin their encounters with demons. These teachings come from Sacred Scripture, the Magisterium, the Fathers of the Church, illuminated saints, and the Doctors of the Church, in particular St. Thomas Aquinas. There are also many rules which must be followed during the course of an exorcism, as stipulated in the Church's Rite of Exorcism. Nonetheless, it is the collective experience of exorcists which has provided them with the greatest concrete tools of the trade. Exorcists know what they know because it has been handed down to them by the previous generation of exorcists. Many of the troubles we are experiencing today are the result of an interruption of the transmission of this knowledge due to the current age of unbelief.

This unbelief unfortunately extends into the hierarchy of the Church herself, as Fr. Thomas points out. Perhaps as a result of the effects of the abuse scandal in the US, many bishops, he says, do not want to get involved in the issue of diabolical activity. There are also only a few bishops who even seem to know much about the practice of exorcisms.[1] A bishop once told Fr. Amorth that he had not appointed any exorcists because he was afraid of the devil. The thought that leaving the devil alone will help keep you safe is the exact opposite of the truth. As Fr. Amorth states, "The more you combat the devil, the more he keeps clear of you!"[2]

As we discussed briefly in Chapter One, the devil loves when we become wounded. It would seem, based on what exorcists have said about the cowardice of some bishops, that the devil is taking advantage of the fear within many bishops that follows the abuse scandal and the subsequent loss of credibility. It may go further than that, though. As Fr. Thomas also said, "Some bishops simply don't believe – they've told me so!"[3] Whether from fear or disbelief, if we do not oppose the devil, he will gain ground against us. As Fr. Amorth said, "The more we fear the devil, the more he attacks us."[4]

As a result of this situation, those priests who are called to be exorcists are not always given the support and encouragement they need and deserve. This, like all things, can be used for the purification of the priest. Fr. Fortea says that God uses this to counter the temptation of pride that may come into the mind of the exorcist as a result of the admiration and thanks he receives from those whom he has helped to liberate. Fr. Fortea states that he does not know of any exorcist who has been spared suspicion and persecution, even from other priests, as a result of the work he does as an exorcist. Most of this comes from a disregard for the practice, believing instead that it belongs buried with other "medieval superstitions."[5]

Seminaries are also lagging behind in the training that priests need for deliverance and exorcism ministry. Since seminaries are overseen by bishops, and given the criticisms stated above, it is no surprise that seminaries are not teaching anything about exorcisms to the men they are forming. As a result, as Fr. Thomas states, newly appointed exorcists are forced to seek out other exorcists for advice on how to proceed with their training. When they do so, it is often in

---

[1] Fr. Thomas #1
[2] Amorth, 115
[3] Fr. Thomas #1
[4] Amorth, 70
[5] Fortea, 102

a spirit of uncertainty, feeling as if they really don't know where to turn or how to begin.[6]

There are more programs slowly emerging in various parts of the world to help train exorcists. However, one of the best things is for new exorcists to attend exorcisms and see the reality of the situation.[7] Fr. Amorth agrees that, in addition to study and shared experience, actual work with exorcisms is vital.[8] Fr. Fortea adds, "The continuous exercise of this ministry gives the exorcist a very specialized and deep knowledge of demons that cannot be learned in any book or school."[9]

Fr. Ripperger says that exorcists tend to network quite a bit, and this begins by studying under other exorcists. Many priests are sent to Rome to study there under priests who have experience in exorcisms dating back several decades. This typically entails not only instruction from experienced exorcists but attending and witnessing numerous exorcisms. Since many priests are unfamiliar with the reality of exorcism and demonic possession, these experiences serve as a significant first step toward gaining the awareness needed for their priestly ministry. Priests who take advantage of these opportunities see that it addresses a certain deficiency in their seminary training.

As part of the networking that supports exorcists in their work, priests will attend exorcism and deliverance conferences all over the world, including in the United States. Many of these conferences are supported by the International Association of Exorcists, officially approved by the Church in 2014, but which began in 1994 under the direction of Fr. Amorth. He said one of the motives behind organizing this association was the value of sharing both experience and theological updates on exorcism ministry.[10]

These conferences give priests opportunities to learn more about the 'art' of casting out demons and to hear stories from expert exorcists. At these conferences, exorcists will share the 'current events' news stories from the world of deliverance ministry. One example, related to me by a priest late in the year 2005, after Pope Benedict had

---

[6] Fr. Thomas #1
[7] Fr. Thomas #1
[8] Amorth, 108
[9] Fortea, 102
[10] Amorth, 114-5

been elected, concerns the election of Pope Benedict. At a conference, an exorcist shared his experience of liberating a person from possession by several demons. At one point in the exorcism, the demons began to talk and complain to one another, almost as if the exorcist was not present in the room anymore. The priest just listened. As they were bemoaning the difficulty they were having at interrupting the election of the new Pope, one demon stated, "SHE keeps getting in the way." The exorcist understood that this was a reference to the protective work which Our Lady was providing for the election process.

An interesting note about these conferences concerns the awareness which the occult world has of these gatherings. One priest related to me that, for a time, these conferences were less strict when it came to those who were permitted to attend, but they had recently, as of, perhaps, 2016, restricted attendance to only those who had been approved and sent by their Bishop. He told me that this was due to the fact that witches had snuck into these conferences, without drawing attention to themselves, and had been, literally, taking notes about what was being discussed. They were attempting to discover what the exorcists had discovered about the workings of the diabolical. With these insights, the witches, and other Satanist groups, could adjust their tactics accordingly. As we can see, the spiritual battle is a real war, and it plays out not only in the invisible realms.

This past May, 2019, the Pontifical Athenaeum Regina Apostolorum hosted an exorcism training course where, for the first time, participants were allowed to attend who came not just from the Church but also from among the Lutherans, Greek Orthodox, Anglicans, and Pentecostals. Father Pedro Barrajón, the Spanish exorcist who was in charge of the event, clearly understood the dangers mentioned above. He said about the event, "We don't open it to everyone, obviously. That would open us up to being infiltrated by devil worshippers, not those trying to fight him. It is not something we think should be taken lightly."[11] Related here, Fr. Thomas points out that exorcists also learn about the workings of the diabolical from people who have come to them after having left Satanic cults.[12]

---

[11] https://www.foxnews.com/world/satanic-vatican-catholics-exorcism-summit
[12] Fr. Thomas #1

The Exorcism as a Classroom

In addition to networking with other exorcists, priests learn more about how the demons operate from their own experiences during exorcisms. As will be discussed more in the next Chapter, when priests are casting out demons from possessed people, the demons often manifest themselves in ways which go beyond what is normal and natural. These extraordinary manifestations of the demonic are glimpses behind the veil, revealing what they are actually fighting against in the spiritual realm. The demons are caught between two desires: to remain hidden, and to take possession of all things on the earth.[13] As a result, they slip up and reveal themselves. As exorcists have said, demons have no virtue and are impulsive; even if they preferred to remain hidden, they cannot resist attacking us. Motivated by vice, they are unstable, despite their otherwise intense dedication to achieving victory through their craftiness.

When exorcists give talks about their experiences, we may forget, or be unaware of, what they went through in order to learn all of these details. In his talks, Fr. Ripperger, for example, makes it clear that extracting this sort of information from the demons is not as simple as it sounds. He uses the term "beatings" to refer to the kind of authoritative commanding that it takes to submit the demon to his demands and reveal what he knows. He can only get the information piece by piece, spaced out by long periods of repeated commands.[14] The information the demon possesses relates to how he got into the person, what it will take to get him out, what the demon's name is, and what his sin was, among other things that may be helpful. The information obtained in an exorcism can also prove to be useful beyond that specific case.

St. Alphonsus Liguori told the story of one exorcism when the devil revealed which sermon, above all others, he despises the most. He said, "Being compelled by exorcisms, the devil once confessed that of all sermons, that which displeased him most was the sermon on avoiding the occasions of sin: and justly; for the devil laughs at all

---

[13] Fr. Ripperger says, in one of his talks, that demons are territorial. Pope Leo XIII, in *Humanum Genus*, speaks of the Kingdom of Satan and its possession and control over all who disobey Our Lord and follow the example of our first parents in heeding the serpent's lies.

[14] Ripperger #6

the resolutions and promises of penitent sinners who remain in the occasion of sin."[15]

A Demon's Personality

Exorcists have learned things about Satan's personality and how it was impacted by his fall. As Fr. Ripperger relates, Satan has revealed to exorcists that "the reason he is the most vile and vicious and evil is because he is the most wounded by his sin."[16] Every demon fell from heaven due to a specific sin and this sin impacts the way they operate on earth. As Fr. Fortea says, "Each demon sinned in a certain way and with a determined intensity."[17] Satan, for example, fell because he did not want to be subject to anyone.[18] This unique sin of each demon is displayed during the exorcism. The demon will manifest "sins of anger, self-worship, and desperation, among others. Each demon has its own psychology and its own way of being."[19]

The Souls of the Damned

Exorcists have also been considering whether or not a damned soul from Hell is capable of possessing a person. Though this appears contrary to sound theological opinion, the consideration has arisen as a result of strange phenomena which exorcists have observed.

During the course of an exorcism, the "possessor," the main demon inside the person, will reveal its primary sin to the priest. Sometimes, the sin mentioned is not a spiritual sin but one, like murder or lust, which must be committed through a body. The sins of demons are always purely spiritual.[20] As Msgr. Glenn states, "In the bad angels themselves there could be no tendency to fleshly sins, but only to such sins as can be committed by a purely spiritual being, and these sins are two only: pride and envy."[21] The confession of a carnal

---

[15] *Preparation for Death*, 319
[16] Ripperger #6
[17] Fortea, 9
[18] Amorth, 18. Cf. also St. Thomas on page 49.
[19] Fortea, 9
[20] Ripperger #6
[21] Glenn, 54

sin by a "demon" is a confusing admission if human souls are not capable of possessing a person. Though demons will obviously lie, they do speak the truth when commanded to, with proper authority, during the rite of exorcism.

Fr. Fortea is one exorcist who holds the belief that souls of the damned can possess people in the same way as demons. In exorcisms, he has seen the possessing entity stand firm in its claim to be a human soul, even under repeated commands, in the Name of Jesus, to tell the truth. This has also happened alongside obedience to commands to kiss a Cross, adding to the veracity of the entity's claim.[22]

Exorcists and theologians are divided on this issue, especially since demons are liars, which Fr. Fortea admits is a source of debate. In the light of their experiences, exorcists are studying the teachings of St. Thomas and the instructions of the Roman Ritual, in particular the exact meaning of the Latin, in order to prudently navigate this complicated element of exorcism ministry.

Blocking Demons

During one exorcism session, when Fr. Ripperger was seeking to cast a demon away from a person's property, which had become infested, he was able to get the demon to reveal that they only have permission to mess with the property, but they have no rights over it.[23] The demon revealed that the person has to clearly state his authority over the property to help break the hold of the demon. Further, the demon told Father that consecrating the property to Our Lady completely blocks the demons from acting on it. As a result, a prayer was written, based on the famous prayer of St. Louis de Montfort for those making a total consecration of themselves to the Blessed Virgin Mary. Father says he has seen much good fruit from people using this prayer.[24]

Exorcists also know that relics and sacramentals will cause pain to a demon. Fr. Amorth says that our devotion to the saints, and the use of their relics, invites their presence into our lives and helps dis-

---

[22] Fortea, 89. Norm 14 of the Rite of Exorcism is a key text, as per the next paragraph.

[23] Ripperger #7

[24] See Appendix for this prayer, called "Consecration of One's Exterior Goods to the Blessed Virgin Mary."

rupt diabolical activity.[25] Fr. Ripperger says that the use of relics increases the pain that the rite of exorcism brings. Once this pain reaches the threshold of what the demon can withstand, he reveals what he knows and what is key to the person's liberation. Exorcists will place these relics directly on areas of the body of the possessed, once they discern that the demon is located there.[26] Sacramentals, like holy water and blessed salt and crucifixes, which carry powerful blessings with them, also cause pain to the demons, and are essential in the exorcism.[27] Fr. Fortea says that, once they realize what bothers the demon the most, the exorcist will focus in on that.[28] He adds that certain signs can torment demons simply by what they symbolize. Clear unblessed water symbolizes purity and cleanliness and an unblessed crucifix still reminds the demons of the victory of Christ on the Cross.[29]

Our Lady, Terror of Demons

Exorcists have learned through experience, as noted above, that Our Lady is the most powerful instrument against the diabolic. When Our Lady shows up during an exorcism, the possession is over. She has, as Fr. Ripperger puts it, "perfect coercive power" over demons.[30] She has no need to discuss the matter with the demon, or request that they leave; if Our Lady comes to send them off, they run without hesitation. The description that Fr. Ripperger gives is quite startling. He says, "You can tell something's going on [inside the possessed]. Our Lady will appear, they will literally see the abyss open up, they will feel the demon getting ripped out, they will see it going down into the abyss, it closes, and she leaves. She literally doesn't have to say a thing. That's how powerful she is." Father once invoked Our Lady during a possession and the demon started panicking, saying, "Oh no, oh no! Not Her!"[31]

---

[25] Amorth, 126
[26] Ripperger #1, #6
[27] See page 132, and following, for more details on these sacramentals.
[28] Fortea, 88
[29] Fortea, 67
[30] Ripperger #7
[31] Ripperger #7

The great saints in the history of the Church have praised these very attributes of Our Lady which exorcists see manifested before them in their work. St. Bonaventure said, "O how the infernal spirits tremble at the very thought of Mary, and of her august name!"[32] In commenting on a passage from Job, Saint Bonaventure states, "Precisely thus do the devils enter a soul in the time of darkness [ignorance]. If suddenly they are overcome by the dawn, that is, if the grace and mercy of Mary enters the soul, its brightness instantly dispels the darkness, and puts the infernal enemies to flight, as if they fled from death."[33] St. Alphonsus Liguori says that it takes but a glance from Mary to terrify the demons, who scatter so quickly from her, "preferring to have their pains redoubled rather than see themselves thus subject to the power of Mary."[34]

When the devil was asked by an exorcist why he feared the Blessed Virgin Mary more than God Himself, Fr. Amorth says the devil responded, "I feel more humiliated being conquered by a simple creature than by God Himself."[35] According to St. Louis de Montfort, it is the humility of Mary which humiliates the devil more than the power of God, which is why the devil fears her "in a certain sense more than God himself."[36] He describes Mary as being as "terrible as an army in battle array to the devil and his followers."[37] In an area near where St. Dominic was preaching, there was a heretic who was possessed by a multitude of devils. At the command of Our Lady, the demons within him were forced to "confess many great and consoling truths concerning devotion to her."[38] During an exorcism, the demons were forced to admit that the power which God has given to Our Lady is so great that they fear "one of her threats more than all their other torments."[39]

---

[32] *Glories of Mary*, 120
[33] *Glories of Mary*, 121
[34] Ibid.
[35] Amorth, 123
[36] *True Devotion*, 52
[37] *True Devotion*, 50
[38] *True Devotion*, 42
[39] *True Devotion*, 52

Discerning the Cause: Medical and Psychological vs. Spiritual

It is recommended that exorcists have a good understanding of psychology so they can better distinguish between psychological problems and true diabolical influence. It is also helpful because, as in cases of diabolical obsession, it is the mind of the person that is most attacked by the actions of the demon. In the realm of diabolical activity, there can often be a similarity between the two, where the peculiar behaviors or thought patterns of the ill person can resemble both causes. The training and experience of exorcists in the realm of psychology greatly helps our understanding of what is the most likely cause of a disturbance by considering a whole host of factors.

Fr. Ripperger says that every form of mental and physical illness can be caused or mimicked by demons, but not all of these are diabolical; some are purely natural.[40] Some cases are clearer than others, such as when the voices a person might be hearing are saying things that have absolutely no bearing on any spiritual or moral matter.[41] Anxiety and panic attacks can be the result of a natural cause or a diabolical cause. The way the person responds to the prayer of the priest is very helpful in discerning this cause. If a natural cause is involved, the prayer should not have an effect, but some relief should come if the cause is diabolical. Most cases of psychological problems are not caused by the diabolical.[42] While in most cases mental illnesses do have a natural cause, because of the way demons operate, by disturbing the mind, diabolical activity can make a person unbalanced and eventually lead to the emergence of a mental illness.[43]

Exorcists have also witnessed that mental illnesses will be present alongside diabolical possession, though they are distinct realities. Just because someone has been proven to have a mental illness, it does not mean they might not also be possessed.[44] According to Fr. Amorth, Padre Pio believed that many people who remained in psychiatric hospitals for the majority of their lives were actually possessed and could have been cured by an exorcism. The Spanish

---

[40] Ripperger #1
[41] Ripperger #6
[42] Ripperger #6
[43] Fortea, 31
[44] Fortea, 98

Carmelite priest Blessed Francis Palau exorcised all of the patients where he worked, which resulted in the cure of many.[45] Fr. Paolo Carlin told the story of a girl who was treated for thirty years as a psychiatric patient but was then liberated from a demon after ten months of weekly prayer with the exorcist.[46] After processing about one hundred and twenty-five cases over six years, Fr. Thomas says that ninety percent of those people were suffering from a mental health issue. It was still beneficial to have seen them, he says, for two reasons: until they speak to an exorcist, the issue remains a mystery, and it is always possible for there to be both a mental and diabolical issue at the same time.[47]

Exorcists look for certain signs, and have noticed certain common elements, that reveal the presence of the diabolical. For example, speaking to the demon in Latin is helpful because the person will not know the specific moment when the demon itself is being addressed. This will help verify or determine whether it is a true case of possession.[48] The presence of any sort of extraordinary phenomena will help distinguish between a mental illness like schizophrenia and possession.[49]

One sign which is apparently a common experience that exorcists have is a diabolical look that manifests in the eyes of the possessed person. This brings to life the common adage, "the eyes are the windows for the soul." This sign, according to Fr. Fortea, could appear as the priest is praying in the beginning of the exorcism. While some people will close their eyes and go into a trance, the other response to the prayers of the priest is for the demon to look at the priest through the eyes of the possessed with, as Father says, "an evil look."[50] Fr. Thomas has had this experience as well. He says, "In the [possessed] person's eyes, there is something like coke-bottle-like contact lenses …superimposed on the person." Having worked in a mortuary, Father says he has seen that there is clearly something absent when

---

[45] Amorth, 86
[46]http://www.catholicdigest.com/news/conversation/an-exorcist-gives-tools-for-spiritual-warfare/
[47] Fr. Thomas #2
[48] Fortea, 81
[49] Fortea, 86
[50] Fortea, 82

looking into the eyes of a corpse. He adds, "Something, the soul, is gone. When you look into the eyes of a person who has a demonic issue, you can often times see the demon in the eyes."[51]

Fr. Ripperger had a similar experience when interacting with a member of a paranormal research group. He could tell the man was possessed due to a certain look the man had, which, as Father says, exorcists can detect.[52] He also tells the story of one woman who was referred to an exorcist by a doctor who thought the person might be possessed. The doctor said that the woman was hearing voices and that there were spirits talking to her. When the doctor asked her more about that, she said that one of the demons was looking at him through her right eye. The doctor then looked at that eye and it immediately turned bright red and then back to the normal color.[53]

Demons are also capable of causing ailments which can appear to be true physical illnesses. One extraordinary example of how demons can do this concerns the man with stage four pancreatic cancer whom Fr. Ripperger visited, and whom we mentioned earlier in the section on diabolical oppression.[54] He prayed the minor exorcism prayers over the man and invoked Our Lady as well. A week later, it was gone, and he was declared free of the pancreatic cancer. People thought that Fr. Ripperger had a gift of healing, but he explained that this was not an extraordinary gift which he possessed, but an indicator that the cause of the illness was diabolical. When the demon was driven away, the illness went with it.[55] Fr. Amorth had a similar thing occur when he liberated a woman who was possessed as the result of a spell. When the demon departed, the woman was also cured of a tumor.[56] When someone thinks they are suffering from a spiritual evil, and feels ill in connection with it, the first thought should be that there is a natural cause. It is only rarely that an illness is caused by the diabolical.[57]

---

[51] Fr. Thomas #2
[52] Ripperger #1
[53] Ripperger #6
[54] See page 39.
[55] Ripperger #6
[56] Amorth, 71
[57] Amorth, 84

Compendium V

+ Exorcists depend on a network of support for their ministries. Seminaries are inadequately preparing priests for this ministry and newly appointed exorcists often struggle to acquire what they need in order to be formed well.
+ Many people in the Church today are afraid, ignorant, or unbelieving regarding the existence of Satan and the necessity of exorcisms.
+ The best way to train an exorcist is for him to witness the reality with his own eyes.
+ Exorcists learn a great deal about their ministry and the work of demons by attending conferences with other exorcists and by hearing stories from what actually happens inside exorcisms.
+ The occult and Satanic groups in the world are aware of the networking of exorcists and seek to infiltrate it to learn what exorcists know.
+ Exorcists have learned how demons think and how they are motivated by different sins as well as the psychology which they each have as individual spirits.
+ Exorcists are studying whether the souls of the damned are capable of possessing people, as a result of certain phenomena observed in exorcisms.
+ Certain sacramentals will frustrate and block the work of demons.
+ Our Lady is a remarkably powerful force against the demonic.
+ Medical and diabolical issues often overlap, and it is important for exorcists to have some background or familiarity with psychology to better navigate the ambiguities of some of the symptoms.
+ Demons are capable of causing mental and physical illnesses, which are distinguished from authentically natural causes by the prayers of the exorcist.
+ Exorcists look for certain signs and phenomena which indicate that a mental or physical illness is actually diabolical in origin.

Chapter Six

Inside the Exorcism

Every person who comes to see an exorcist is put through an intense vetting process to determine what medical, psychological, and spiritual problems they have, if any. If there is a demonic presence involved, there is usually something that does not fit with the other details acquired, and which does not match with purely psychological problems. It is only after this process that an exorcism will begin. Fr. Amorth says that he does not accept anyone who has not first received a psychiatric evaluation.[1] After this evaluation, there are usually clear indicators that point the priest toward the possibility of diabolical influence. Fr. Amorth saw a boy who was being treated by a psychiatrist and whose possession prevented him from sleeping. At one point, the boy was given "enough sleep medication to sedate an elephant" but was still unable to sleep. This was an indicator that it was time to turn to a priest.[2]

Out of one hundred and fifty cases in a year, only about three people were actually possessed, from Fr. Ripperger's experience.[3] Fr. Grob said that about eighty-five percent of people who come to him don't need an exorcism, though they may benefit from a priest.[4] For Fr. Thomas, only ten percent of the people he saw had an issue of the diabolical.[5] The rate of obsession is much higher than that of possession. Fr. Ripperger estimates that about twenty-five percent of people in this country are diabolically obsessed.[6]

---

[1] Amorth, 84
[2] Amorth, 85
[3] Ripperger #2
[4] Fr. Grob video
[5] Fr. Thomas #2
[6] Ripperger #1, #6

Praying over the person will reveal whether there is anything demonic involved. Fr. Amorth has seen that certain spirits, such as "the spirit of anger, vengeance, impurity, or suicide," will cause particular reactions in the possessed. These can emerge as easily as during the initial interview of the exorcist with the possessed, or during a simple prayer of liberation.[7] Though it is rare, the possessed will sometimes react with screams or violent contortions as soon as they see the exorcists, or at the moment the exorcist lays his hand on the possessed. The demon's preference is to remain hidden but, "no matter how hard he strives to hide his reactions, in the end he must give in."[8]

Fr. Fortea warns about this same possibility of a violent reaction, which is a startling indicator of a true possession. He says that, while it is recommended that the priest pray with his eyes closed at the beginning of the exorcism, so as to remain focused on the prayer, someone, if not the priest, must keep an eye on the possessed person so they do not lunge at him.[9]

The time it takes for a case of possession to be resolved can vary. Fr. Ripperger says that some cases of possession will last until the end of the person's earthly life, but most can be resolved in two to three months. He says a more intense approach is helpful, which slowly breaks the defenses of the demon and weakens it. This would include meeting on a daily basis, for about three to six hours a day. This intense approach can bring about a liberation within a week.[10] Fr. Amorth says he usually sees a person once a month, and more frequently if necessary.[11]

Fr. Fortea says that there are two reasons why an exorcism might take longer than expected. First, the priest typically instructs the possessed on adopting the proper spiritual works that are needed in order to eradicate those things in their soul that the demon can latch on to. If the possessed is being disobedient to these instructions, the demon will not be as easy to remove. Second, the inexperience of the exorcist might also be slowing down the liberation process. If that is the

---

[7] Amorth, *More Stories*, 115
[8] Amorth, *More Stories*, 109
[9] Fortea, 82
[10] Ripperger #1
[11] Amorth, 101

case, this exorcist should bring in another exorcist with more experience, particularly with the kind of demon involved.[12]

Exorcists receive the assistance of devout laymen to help them in the exorcism. Fr. Ripperger says that he begins his exorcisms by praying over these people who are helping him.[13] This assistance could include holding down the possessed, protecting the priest from any violent outbursts from the possessed, protecting the possessed person from harming himself during the manifestation, praying for the exorcist and the possessed, and informing the exorcist of any information that the Holy Spirit may impart to them pertinent to the liberation of the possessed.

Fr. Amorth says it is critical that these qualified individuals have a strong spiritual life and the ability to handle all that may transpire in the exorcism. They also must not be "easily impressionable" such that they do not fall for the devil's tricks.[14] Fr. Ripperger says he only uses people who are over 55, devout, stable, and have no children at home.[15] When he was gathering his team together, as a new exorcist, Fr. Randall Weber said he looked for the same qualities one looks for in an exorcist: piety, deep faith, recourse to Confession, etc.[16]

Those who work in exorcism ministry agree that Our Lord protects the priest and those who assist at exorcisms from the demon, unless that person is committing mortal sins. Two stories will help illustrate this protection.

A priest friend of mine related a fascinating, and somewhat frightening, story. Here, too, it is important to point out that we need not fear the demons. In Christ, we are stronger than they are. Of course, on our own, in our sins, without His grace, we are weaker than they are, and are easy prey for them. This story concerns a person who confronted a demon in a state of mortal sin. At a certain exorcism, a layman was helping by holding down the possessed person. He stood near his shoulder and held down his arm to keep him from flailing about during the exorcism. At one point, the priest and others in attendance noticed that the possessed and the layman holding his

---

[12] Fortea, 109

[13] Ripperger #1

[14] Amorth, 110

[15] Ripperger #1

[16] Weber video

arm down had both become oddly quiet. Then, they heard a faint squeaky voice come from the nearly motionless lips of the layman, saying, "Help...me..." The priest and others noticed that the possessed man had locked his eyes on the layman's eyes and the layman was completely frozen. With great effort, and after covering the eyes of the possessed and the eyes of the layman, the people at the exorcism pulled the layman away from the possessed man. Afterward, it became clear that the demon was trying to also possess the layman. This was more understandable when the layman admitted that he had an unconfessed mortal sin. This had made him an easy target for the demon.

A story told by Adam Blai depicts the opposite of the above situation. He was helping at an exorcism, in a similar manner as the layman in the above story. He was helping to hold down the possessed person while the priest was working against the demon. As he used his physical strength to keep the possessed man still, he reflected on the nature of the battle in which he found himself, and realized he was taking the wrong approach. He knew it was the power of Christ, which resided also in him, which was the source of victory over the demonic, and not his own strength. He then slowly lessened the amount of pressure he was using to hold the man down, going from two forceful hands to just one. Eventually, he was only holding the man down with his fingertips. In the end, by invoking God and the holy angels, he simply prayed and the possessed man stayed still.[17] This illustrates the statement of Fr. Amorth, "Faith matters a great deal in the exorcist's work."[18] It also calls to mind the statement of Our Lord, "This kind cannot be driven out by anything but prayer and fasting."[19]

Signs of Possession

As the exorcism proceeds, the task of the exorcist is to find out several things: how the demon got in, who they are, how many there are, what is the time of the person's liberation, and what will be the

---

[17] Blai, 100
[18] Amorth, 107
[19] Mark 9:29

cause of the liberation. All the way through the process, the person will suffer from horrible diabolic obsession and oppression.[20]

The priest will look for signs that indicate the person is truly possessed by a demon. One of the first indicators, as exorcists seem to all experience, is that, as soon as the priest begins the rite, the possessed person will go into a trance and lose consciousness.[21] Some of the other signs will manifest in the life of the person, and others will manifest during the exorcism itself. For a demon to manifest, it simply means that the demon, who typically remains hidden, becomes the main actor in the person's body, and speaks and behaves in manners that are clearly diabolical and beyond normal human capabilities. There are four main signs that a person is possessed.[22]

Aversion to the sacred. Diabolical aversion to the sacred is commonly held to be an aspect of true possession, though not beyond doubt. This could also be from a negative experience or from psychological issues or psychological aversions, and not necessarily due to the diabolical.[23] Sometimes, aversion to the sacred is the first indicator, to the possessed person, that there is an issue of possession. It could appear when they come in contact, even just visually, with something sacred.[24] The reaction can range from slight annoyance to a full rage at the sight or presence of the sacred.[25] Visiting sacred shrines has been, in some cases, the cause for the manifestation of a demon which had remained hidden up until that moment.[26]

Which sacred thing or Sacrament a demon is specifically most sensitive to will vary from demon to demon. This is also related to the nature of their fall and the sin which was committed in their rejection of God. Certain demons are able to tolerate some sacred things but not others.[27] In the documentary on the true story behind the

---

[20] Ripperger #6

[21] For example, Amorth, 66

[22] Though there are similarities, these manifestations differ from the spiritual gifts given to someone like St. Bernadette, who had knowledge about the Immaculate Conception, but did not understand it; the Apostles, who spoke in tongues by the power of the Holy Spirit; and St. Joseph of Cupertino, who levitated frequently.

[23] Ripperger #6

[24] Amorth, 82

[25] Fortea, 72

[26] Amorth, 69

[27] Ripperger #6

movie *The Exorcist*, the possessed boy was able to be baptized and receive Holy Communion, but the demon remained. Confession, for example, drives out evil from the soul, while the exorcism only drives evil out of the body. When the possessed goes to Confession, which exorcists say is much more powerful than the exorcism itself, it does great damage to the hold that the demon has on the possessed, but does not always cause the liberation.

In this category is also the ability to detect the sacred, even if the sacred object is hidden. The demon, for example, will be able to identify relics in the rooms and blessed medals worn by the exorcist.[28]

Occult knowledge. Some of the possessed have a knowledge of things about which they should know nothing at all. This kind of knowledge could include events in the lives of others, what's happening in a neighboring house, what the priest was doing in between the sessions of the exorcism, certain scientific truths, and theological concepts, the latter two being beyond the person's competency. Fr. Ripperger worked with a woman who had become attached to the demon inside of her because the demon would give her secret knowledge about her husband.[29] In another story, a woman, who had less than a high school education, was able to articulate, clearly and properly, a theological concept which only the most studied of theologians understood.[30] Fr. Cesare Truqui told the story of a woman who, after receiving a blessing from the priest, had a vision where she was able to see a specific object in another country in her family home in great detail which had otherwise been completely unknown to her.[31]

Speaking in an unknown language. This sign of possession is knowledge of languages completely foreign to the possessed person and of which they could have no working knowledge. Like the angels, demons have infused knowledge of all languages. Demons are capable of speaking all languages with ease and mastery. In its manifestation, this sign leaves no room for the common doubt which says

---

[28] Blai, 71
[29] Ripperger #6
[30] Ripperger #2
[31] Fr. Truqui video

that the possessed heard the foreign language at one point and is simply reciting what little they know.

In an exorcism, the person might be able to understand foreign languages and "obey orders given in Latin, Greek, Hebrew and other languages, even when used simultaneously."[32] Adam Blai recounts the possession of a person with only a high-school education where the demon "correctly responded to questions in English, French, Latin, Lithuanian, and German."[33] Fr. Ripperger relates that in one exorcism, the demon would only speak in Latin, and was so particular about proper grammar that he would not respond to the priest if the priest's grammar was incorrect.[34] Adam Blai has also seen this behavior from a demon. The demons also mock the inability of translators to catch subtle nuances of a language when doing the translation.[35]

This sign is a prime example of how demons are inclined to invert everything sacred. Pentecost was the first great miracle and manifestation of the Church at its birth following the Ascension of Our Lord into Heaven. At that moment, St. Peter was able to speak in a language that was intelligible to people from over a dozen different countries. It makes sense that the demons would mock this divine gift. Further, as Adam Blai has seen, demons appear to have their own version of "tongues," which, as he says, is "very disturbing to hear and hard to describe; it is a kind of hissing, lilting language."[36]

Strengths beyond one's natural capacity. Demons can sometimes manifest through the person by exhibiting superhuman strength. Fr. Ripperger relates the story of a ten year old boy who was possessed and who, during the exorcism, when the demon manifested, was able to lift the priest and another man off the ground.[37] The strength that can accompany the manifestation of a demon can even include lifting several people off of the ground all at once.[38] Fr. Amorth was told of an exorcism where the possessed was a young

---

[32] Fortea, 87
[33] Blai, 69
[34] Ripperger #2
[35] Blai, 70
[36] Blai, 70
[37] Ripperger #2
[38] Fortea, 87

girl, tied down with leather straps, but who still required four strong men to hold her down, and with difficulty. He witnessed a case of a young girl who was almost able to resist the efforts of seven strong assistants who sought to hold her still during the exorcism.[39]

This manifestation does not just occur during the performance of the exorcism. Fr. Truqui told the story of a man who realized he was possessed when he was praying on a retreat. The man entered into a trance suddenly and a friend he was with touched him just to make sure he was alright. At that moment, the possessed man grabbed the friend with one hand and threw him away in the other direction, in a manner that is completely impossible for a normal person to do.[40]

Fr. Amorth notes that a "demented person in an insane asylum can be immobilized with a straitjacket," but a demoniac is capable of snapping even iron chains. Fr. Candido Amantini, the teacher of Fr. Amorth, reported a case of a frail young girl who manifested the same strengths as the Gerasene demoniac from the Gospel of Mark. As Fr. Amorth recalls, "She broke every bond, even some heavy leather straps with which they tried to tie her down. Once, when she was tied with strong ropes to an iron bed, she broke some of the iron rods and folded others at a right angle."[41]

This sign of possession includes not just manifestations of strength but also things like levitation. Some priests witness levitation during their initial training. Fr. Ripperger stated that he has only seen levitation twice in ten years, though other exorcists see it more frequently.[42] A man levitated just as Fr. Amorth placed his hand on the man's shoulder at the beginning of the exorcism. Even though five people were trying, they could not hold him down.[43]

This sign of possession can often provoke fear in people, but it is good to remember that Our Lord oversees all the activity of the demons. Further, as Fr. Amorth says, it is only in the most violent cases that the person actually needs to be strapped down.[44] As Adam Blai

---

[39] Amorth, 66
[40] Fr. Truqui video
[41] Amorth, *Exorcist Tells*, 70
[42] Ripperger #6
[43] Amorth, 103
[44] Amorth, 103

points out, in some cases, the possessed person is completely compliant and does not need any restraint.[45]

Fr. Ripperger adds a fascinating detail about the sort of manifestations that exorcists witness. He says that the most common form of diabolical manifestation, in nearly every case of possession, is what he calls "morphing," where the person begins to change shape as the demon manifests. It seems that this is typically a change in the person's facial structure. Some demons will manifest in the exact same way each time, but others are not predictable in that regard. The demon Beelzebub, for example, always manifests in the same way. Here, in the body of the possessed, Father says, "The jaw extends out about two inches on each side, the head narrows, the eyes come together and they turn bloodshot."[46] Fr. Thomas has seen similar contortions of the body of the possessed, sometimes, as he says, moving in a manner that resembles a serpent. "The demons," he adds, "will move peoples' bodies in ways that seem unimaginable."[47]

Stages of Liberation

The liberation of the person is something that happens progressively as the possessed and the exorcist work together to expel the demons. Typically, there are about six stages in the process, but some of these are skipped if the exorcism moves more quickly. Before the liberation can occur, the exorcist must have acquired control over the demon.[48]

After the presence of the demonic has been verified in the person, the work moves to getting the demon to come to the surface so the exorcist can then begin the process of removing the demon. The Gospel of Mark states that there are different kinds of demons.[49] This is partly witnessed by exorcists in the fact that demons will interact with them in two basic manners: open and closed. Open demons will begin manifesting as soon as the rite begins. Closed demons tend to hide and are harder to discover. Demons are showy, though, and like

---

[45] Blai, 71
[46] Ripperger #2
[47] Fr. Thomas #2
[48] Ripperger #6
[49] Mark 9:28

to show off to other demons, so most will manifest eventually.[50] There are also hidden demons who give no signs of their presence in a person, deceiving even a very experienced exorcist. For these demons, as Fr. Fortea says, the priest needs to be more insistent in his prayers, but it typically only takes a few additional minutes to get the demon to respond.[51]

When the demon is open, it is, of course, easier to proceed. They will begin speaking right away but will also try to distract the priest by dismissing the person's issues as being purely psychological. Since this will be done in the voice of the possessed, not a diabolical voice, it will clearly be a sign of the demon's effort to deceive the priest. It will also be an obvious indicator of the demonic because this statement will be a complete reversal of the attitude of the person, who did not, prior to that moment, believe the problems were psychological. The person will also laugh at everything the priest is doing during the exorcism. These demons can sometimes be violent as well and often need to be held down.[52]

Closed demons try to hide and not reveal their presence, even when the priest has begun praying over the possessed. The priest will have to look for some of the subtle manifestations which will be occurring. He should be looking for things like the eyes being rolled back beneath the closed eyelids.[53] This is a common sign of the manifestation of the demon. Some closed demons, though, are completely mute. These, as Fr. Amorth says, are the most difficult to address.[54]

This behavior from the open and closed demons is what Fr. Ripperger describes as the second stage in the process of liberating the person. He calls this stage obfuscation.[55] Obfuscation means "to make obscure, confusing, or bewildering." As the priest continues with the prayers, the manifestation will become more obvious and the demon will end this game of hiding.

Fr. Ripperger describes the third stage as the battle phase, where the priest is slowly gaining power over the demon. Here, the demon

---

[50] Ripperger #6
[51] Fortea, 78, 81
[52] Fortea, 76
[53] Fortea, 76
[54] Amorth, 67
[55] Ripperger #6, #1

will attack the priest interiorly, in a way that resembles what the possessed person is experiencing. This attack reveals a lot about the demon, which the exorcist can then use against the demon. Father says that, if the exorcist is very experienced, the demons are more cautious about taking this approach.[56]

In this stage of the process, a rare fourth stage may emerge, where the demon begins to lose control and lash out with external manifestations of his power. This can include moving and throwing things in the room. One woman that Fr. Ripperger helped had a demon of destruction which would manifest throughout the exorcism and destroy things like the plumbing and the hard drive on the pastor's computer.[57] In the true story behind *The Exorcist* movie, items were being tossed around the room during the exorcism.

Just before the liberation, in the fifth stage of the process, the exorcist now has control over the demon after having acquired the information critical to liberating the person. The demon is much more subdued at this point and tends to manifest only during the exorcism sessions. As a result, the life of the possessed person is much more normal. One of the things the exorcist needs to know, which he has at this point, is the number and names of the demons present.[58] The exorcist also needs to know how the demon came into the person. This will play a role in the method of getting the demon out.

Bonds can be formed with demons in many ways, even, as Fr. Amorth states, in ways that are subtle and almost unconscious. These can occur through a naïve curiosity, particularly when exposed to something tied even loosely to the occult. This can occur more easily if it is also combined with, for example, a personal desire to know the future.[59] Some people will explicitly invite possession, not only through the practice of magic and satanic worship, but also through a curiosity which is no longer naïve.[60]

The importance of the names of the demons, as Fr. Thomas describes, is connected to the issue of a person's call. As he says, in Baptism, the priest asks the name given to the child in an analogous

---

[56] Ripperger #6, #1
[57] Ibid.
[58] Ibid.
[59] Amorth, *More Stories*, 114
[60] Blai, 62

way to how God called the prophets by name and Our Lord called the Apostles by name. By this direct call, by name, it was a personal call, and one which drew them into the Kingdom of God and of the light. A demon resists revealing his name because he prefers to dwell in the darkness and, as Father adds, because they are liars and deceivers. Conveying what all exorcists seem to think, Fr. Carlin says, "The Devil's best trick is that of persuading man that he does not exist."[61] All demons do this, in order that, through their hiddenness, they may continue their evil work. Fr. Thomas continues, "Once the exorcist gets the name of the demon, the demon begins to lose his power because he is then being called into the realm of the light. It's like bringing a fish out of water. Demons will come at this point because they are legalists and the exorcist has the authority."[62]

Fr. Amorth mentions, as Fr. Ripperger also did in Chapter One, that there are certain demons who are more central, powerful, and difficult to deal with. He states that, if the demon's name is a biblical name or one given in Tradition, like Satan, Beelzebub, Lucifer, Zebulun, Meridian, or Asmodeus, "we are dealing with 'heavyweights' who are much tougher to defeat." In agreement with Fr. Thomas, he adds that the revelation of the demon's name is a good sign. When the demon reveals this, it greatly weakens his power.[63]

The final things the exorcist seeks are the time and date of the demon's exit and the sign they will give to indicate they have departed.[64] As was discussed earlier,[65] Our Lord strictly regulates what the demons are allowed to do, and even restricts how long they are allowed to stay. The demons know the time during the exorcism at which they must depart and cannot disobey that command. The demons also give a sign, or obey a final command, after which they depart from the possessed person. Fr. Amorth states that, as the time of his departure approaches, the demon's actions will begin to reveal that it is near. Though, at the beginning of the exorcism, the demon will have stated that he will never depart, he will then indicate that his departure is "soon." Sometimes, the demon will reveal to the exorcist

---

[61] Carlin, 7
[62] Fr. Thomas #2
[63] Amorth, 102. Similarly, see page 10.
[64] Ripperger #6
[65] See Chapter Four.

the date of the departure. Often, this is a lie, but it is also often true, due to Our Lord's control over the demon.[66]

In the documentary about the true story behind the movie *The Exorcist,* the demon in the possessed boy states that he must say one word, and the demon will leave, but that the boy would never say it. Eventually, and remarkably, St. Michael appeared vocally within the boy and commanded the demon to leave and used the one word which the boy needed to utter for the demon to leave. That word was "Dominum," which, in Latin, means Lord. When St. Michael used the term, the demon departed, and the liberation was accomplished. Fr. Fortea stated that demons of the highest order are often cast out only by the involvement of an angel toward the end of the exorcism.[67]

The final stage of the process is referred to as the liberation of the person, which is the purpose of the exorcism rite. When the last demon has left the person, Fr. Fortea says the person "remains at peace, recovers consciousness, and opens his eyes. He may even feel a spiritual happiness." To be certain that the demon is gone, the priest should pray for a few more minutes. If there is still a demon, it will begin to manifest again.[68] This is something that will occasionally happen. Demons like to hide and give the impression that they have departed. They also tend to attempt a return and restart their attack on the person. Fr. Amorth states that an occasional exorcism after the liberation can be beneficial for the person in order to counter the demon's persistence.[69]

After being liberated, the person typically does not have any serious lingering effects but is able to return to a normal life.[70] A person who has been exorcised only needs to worry about becoming possessed again if they return to living in a state of sin. One or two mortal sins, within the context of a practicing Christian life, will not cause the return of possession. However, if they do abandon the Christian life after liberation, the second possession would be "by more and worse demons."[71]

---

[66] Amorth, *More Stories,* 137f
[67] Fortea, 110
[68] Fortea, 106
[69] Amorth, *Exorcist Tells,* 100
[70] Amorth, 83
[71] Fortea, 107

Fr. Fortea had one lady return to him, after being successfully liberated from all of her demons, saying she was experiencing signs of demonic activity in her body again. She had been faithfully praying and living her Christian life since being liberated just a few days prior. When Fr. Fortea met with her, it only took a few minutes of prayer to alleviate the demonic influence. He discerned that the demon, which rarely happens, was trying to re-possess her, but her spiritual life was literally functioning like armor against the demon. After these final prayers, she had no further problems.[72]

The importance of not relapsing into a life of grave sin was emphasized to St. Bridget by Our Lady. As recorded by St. Alphonsus, Our Lady revealed that, "if the soul does not amend and obliterate its sins by sorrow, the devils almost immediately return and continue to possess it."[73]

---

[72] Fortea, 107
[73] *Glories of Mary* 124

Compendium VI

+ Cases of possession are rare. Less than ten percent of people who come to see an exorcist have a true case of possession.
+ When a priest prays over a person, if a demon is present, it will manifest in some way. Some manifestations are subtle while others are obvious.
+ The time it takes for a person to be liberated varies greatly and depends on many factors including the spiritual work done by the possessed to aid the liberation.
+ Exorcists depend on the support of a team of devout Catholics to assist them at exorcisms.
+ There are four classic signs that a person is possessed: aversion to the sacred, secret knowledge, fluency in unknown languages, superhuman strength.
+ Demons are able to manipulate the body of the possessed in quite startling ways during the exorcism.
+ The liberation is a slow process that requires forcing the demon to communicate and acquiring the information necessary to gain control over the demon.
+ After liberation, it is critical that the person protect his spiritual life so as not to relapse into sin and suffer a worse re-possession.

Chapter Seven

Authority and the Diabolical

The coat of arms of Vatican City is designed in such a way so as to convey the power and authority which the Church has received from Our Lord. It contains, in part, a gold key and a silver key that cross over each other. These keys refer to the power of Orders and the power of jurisdiction: the priesthood and faculties, ordination and the power to use it.[1] The gold key represents the power in the Kingdom of God and the silver key represents the authority of the papacy on earth. Not only does a priest need to receive Holy Orders through ordination, but he must also receive permissions from his bishop to function as a priest. This extends even more so to exorcisms and administering the Sacrament of Confirmation, both of which a priest is capable of doing, but only with the permission of his bishop.[2]

We see in the Gospel of Mark that Our Lord gives the Apostles both power and authority over demons. These two are distinct aspects of exorcism ministry. For example, in Mark 9:28, the Apostles, possessing authority over the demons, are not able to cast it out as a result of a lack of "prayer and fasting." Prayer and fasting, holiness in general, increases the efficacy of the exorcism. This distinction is also seen in Mark 9:38 when a man is seen by the Apostles to be casting out demons even though he is not one of the Twelve. This man had the power to cast out demons but had not been given the authority.[3]

As all exorcists say, demons are very legalistic and know when someone has authority and when they do not. If the person commanding the demons truly possesses the proper authority, the demons will

---

[1] Ripperger #4
[2] A priest is capable of administering Confirmation, without stated permission, in an emergency.
[3] Fortea, 105

obey. If the person does not, it can take a dangerous turn. It is useful to recall, in this context, the story of the Jewish exorcists who sought to imitate St. Paul's exorcism of demons by the invocation of the Name of Jesus. In Acts 19, verses 11-17, we read:

> And God did extraordinary miracles by the hands of Paul, so that handkerchiefs or aprons were carried away from his body to the sick, and diseases left them and the evil spirits came out of them. Then some of the itinerant Jewish exorcists undertook to pronounce the name of the Lord Jesus over those who had evil spirits, saying, "I adjure you by the Jesus whom Paul preaches." Seven sons of a Jewish high priest named Sceva were doing this. But the evil spirit answered them, "Jesus I know, and Paul I know; but who are you?" And the man in whom the evil spirit was leaped on them, mastered all of them, and overpowered them, so that they fled out of that house naked and wounded. And this became known to all residents of Ephesus, both Jews and Greeks; and fear fell upon them all; and the name of the Lord Jesus was extolled.

Fr. Ripperger says that demons, when confronted by one without faculties, will say, "Where's your authority?" and not cooperate. He recounted a case in New York where a group of Protestants tried to perform an exorcism on a person who was possessed and levitating, at times sticking to the ceiling. They were violently attacked and "beaten within an inch of their lives" by the demon within the possessed person who all the while proclaimed, "You have no authority." They called in a Catholic priest, with faculties, and he resolved the situation.[4]

As mentioned earlier, acquiring the name of the demon and the sin that was the cause of his fall, are critical aspects of gaining authority over the demon. Knowledge of the door that was used, the sin which was committed by the person, through which the demon entered, is also critical. Once this sin is exposed, the person can then bring it to Confession and begin the healing process necessary to close the wound which the sin created. That wound is the means for

---

[4] Ripperger #1

the demon to stay latched on to the person. As the healing occurs, the demon further loses his grip.

When exorcists acquire the name of a demon, they are able to use that name in assisting the possessed, even if they do not yet have the proper faculties and permissions to proceed with a formal exorcism. As Fr. Thomas mentioned, using the name of the demon calls the demon into the light to face the Church's authority. If the demon comes forth, but does not meet an authoritative person, it could be dangerous. Laymen as a result, if they, for some reason, come to know the name of a demon involved in a possession case, must not use the name in any way. Fr. Ripperger references the issue of the *Harry Potter* books, which use, for some characters, the names of actual demons that exorcists have encountered. Using the name of a demon outside of the authoritative structure of the rite of exorcism, and when the demon is not being confronted and opposed, actually empowers him as the use of his name in that manner gives him glory in this world.[5]

The Role of the Father

True authority is not a matter that is restricted to the Church alone but is also present within the family. The father, as the head of the family, plays a critical role, including serving as a shepherd and a gatekeeper. This role can lead to blessings for the family, but, if the father neglects to properly wield his authority, it can lead to problems.

The father's headship gives him the authority to bless his family, including his wife and his children. The mother shares in the authority of the father to a certain extent. She is able to bless her children like the father, but she is not able to bless the father, since he has headship over the whole family. The creation of Eve helps explain this difference. As St. Thomas explains, Eve was created from the rib of Adam for a specific reason. By doing so, it showed that they were equal, as she was taken from his own flesh; that she was not his slave, since she was not created from his feet; but that she was not in authority over him, since she was not created from his head.[6] This manner

---

[5] Ripperger #3
[6] Summa 1, Q. 92, A 3

of the creation of Eve thus demonstrates the authority structure within the family as a divinely instituted hierarchy.

Given their origin and their angelic nature, the demons know about the authority structure within the Church and also within families. As a result, the family becomes a special target of the demons, and the father in particular. Fr. Truqui[7] said that there is a demon who specifically targets families, which he sees in many exorcisms. The demon's name is Asmodeus and he is first seen in Sacred Scripture in the book of Tobit. There, he is responsible for orchestrating the deaths of seven husbands of Sarah. As exorcists similarly witness in their work, this major demon was finally driven out by the work of an archangel, St. Raphael.

The entrance of a demon into a family can happen as a result of the disregard for the responsibilities that flow from the father's authority, either by the father himself, or by the mother or children. Like exorcisms, which depend on authority, the proper use of the authority of the father has a real effect on the family.[8] Fathers should thus be concerned about both the material and the spiritual well-being of their families, and see themselves as capable of, and thus responsible for, protecting them in these two ways. The father, then, like Saint Joseph, who bears the title "Terror of Demons," can be a true means of warding off diabolical influence in the family.

Sin involves rejecting the commands of God and, as a consequence, placing ourselves out of the proper structure of authority and in a state where we are vulnerable to evil. Remember how many times Israel was punished by God for infidelity. Israel created a vulnerability by pushing God, and His powerful protection, away. Their enemies were then able to easily make their approach and Israel suffered grave harm. When we go to Confession, we place ourselves back into fidelity to God's covenant and under His protection again.[9]

Generational spirits can enter through the father's authority, as is demonstrated in the book of Exodus, when the Lord says that He will visit "the iniquity of the fathers upon the children to the third and the

---

[7] https://cruxnow.com/global-church/2017/10/28/exorcist-says-theres-demon-targets-family/
[8] Ripperger #1
[9] Ibid.

fourth generation of those who hate me."[10]   Though the mother can also bring evil into the family, as with Eve, the target, even with Eve, is the father, whose authority is universal over the family.   When the father commits a mortal sin of a certain sort, like pornography, he is now vulnerable to diabolical influence.   If a demon comes in at that moment, he can corrupt the whole family, since he entered through the head of the family.[11]   The demon can also remain and be passed down through successive generations.

Binding Prayers and Authority

Laymen are permitted to use what are called "binding prayers" within the proper authority structure. This functions in a similar way to imparting blessings. Parents can bless their children, tracing the Sign of the Cross with their thumb on the forehead of the child, and using a commanded prayer saying, "God bless you," and then a blessing is given. This is done over the children in the same way that a priest can bless everyone.[12]   While the wife is not able to bless her husband, she is permitted to pray binding prayers over him. Each spouse can offer prayers of deliverance for the other spouse as well as on the children.[13]

Though the concept of binding prayers is not well known among Catholics, it has always been in the Tradition of the Church. Like many other traditional teachings, Catholics today have been cut off from knowledge of this aspect of the spiritual life. In a similar way to deliverance ministry, Protestants have picked up this approach and have made it their own. As a result, many Catholics see it as something Protestant.   Fr. Ripperger emphasizes that exorcisms, deliverance ministry, and binding prayers are not of Protestant origin, but are part of the rich heritage of spiritual treasures in the Catholic Faith. That being said, Catholics must learn the proper way to engage in these spiritual works, so they stay in the authoritative structure willed by God and stay out of spiritual trouble.

---

[10] Exodus 20:5
[11] Ripperger #8. Generational spirits are not a defined teaching of the Church.
[12] Ripperger #7
[13] Amorth, 90

There are two prominent mentions of binding demons in the Bible. The first one appears in the Old Testament in the Book of Tobit. Here, the archangel St. Raphael was sent to both heal and to bind a demon. The demon Asmodeus had been responsible for the deaths of the seven husbands of Sarah. Through the binding of Asmodeus, Sarah is freed to safely marry Tobias. In addition to healing Tobit of blindness, this binding of the demon is also referred to as a healing.[14]

In the Gospel of Matthew, Our Lord says, "How can one enter into a strong man's house, and spoil his goods, except he first bind the strong man? and then he will spoil his house."[15] St. Thomas Aquinas presents the understanding of this passage, collecting the wisdom of the great minds in the Church. He says that Our Lord has entered the house of Satan, the "strong man," and has bound him. Thus conquered, Satan is unable to defend his spoils and Our Lord has taken them away. These spoils are the souls who have been bound by the demons. Our Lord comes not to simply bind the demons but the prince of demons also. By thus casting out all the demons, He is also prophesying that He "will take away all error out of the world, and dissolve the craft of the Devil; and He says not rob, but spoil, showing that He will do it with power." This binding also means that He has "taken away from him all power of hindering the faithful from following Christ, and gaining the kingdom of heaven."[16]

Satan and all the demons are thus bound by Our Lord. Like the gift of salvation, and the victory of the Cross, the binding of demons is playing out in time and throughout history. Our Lord gave all mankind the power to be saved but this must be accepted by all men. Likewise, His conquering of Satan was definitive, but it plays out in time and through the ministry of the Church. In our own lives, in Christ and with the power of His Most Precious Blood and His Holy Name, we participate in the conquering of the devil. First, though, we must fight him. Thus, through the binding prayer, we engage in this spiritual struggle with the forces of darkness, knowing that we are the victorious army.

---

[14] Tobit 3:16-17
[15] Matthew 12:29
[16] St. Thomas Aquinas, *Catena Aurea*, Gospel of Matthew 12

It is helpful, then, to think about binding prayers first on the individual level. Here they function as a sort of self-exorcism, where we cast away the demons that are coming against us. We have authority over ourselves in this regard. As a result, when you sense a diabolical influence against you, even as a simple temptation, you can speak directly against the demon in the Name of Jesus. Jesus is still the one with the authority, so the binding prayer must be done in His Name. The binding prayer is, "In the Name of Jesus, I bind you, spirit of N., and I cast you to the foot of the Cross to be judged by Our Lord." The ending could also be, "...to receive your sentence." Fr. Ripperger says that you can add invocations to the prayer, inserting "by the power of the Precious Blood," or "through the intercession of Saint Joseph," for example.[17]

Outside of ourselves, we have authority over others within the proper authority structure established by God. The father in the family has authority over his entire family. The wife shares in that authority but does not have the same headship as the father. With binding prayers, though, the wife is able to pray them for her husband. They may both pray these for their children. Fr. Ripperger says that, while children do not have authority to bless their parents, exorcists have noticed that children can do binding prayers over their parents, due to some aspect of the 4th Commandment. There seems to be a protection over the children that permits them to do this prayer, perhaps "since there are times when the children may have to take care of their parents in old age."[18]

When you are praying for someone outside of the authority structure, the binding prayer may be prayed in an indirect manner. The wording would change to, "O Jesus, I ask You to bind the spirit of N...." Fr. Ripperger recommends this prayer for many reasons and says he has seen a lot of success in its use. This can be prayed for many purposes, such as to drive away demons who are bringing bad friends into a person's life, or bad relationships, or preventing them from converting. Demons can stir up evil people and motivate them to enter your life or refuse to leave your life. This type of friendship can be the source of evil in a child's life and in their mind, through

---

[17] Ripperger #7
[18] Ibid.

which the demon can pull the child away from the family and the Faith. Fr. Ripperger gives a version of the binding prayer to parents to help break up bad relationships.[19] Demons can also interfere with the grace of conversion and attempt to block a person's consent to it. They can fuel the pride and arrogance of an atheist or someone who refuses to enter the Church despite seeing that it is the intellectually proper course to take.[20]

The ability to challenge the devil is something we can do on the natural level. The battle against Satan is a condition of human existence. As a result, God permits us to wield a varying degree of authority against the demons in this battle, even if we are away from Christ to one degree or another. Fr. Ripperger mentions, in one of his talks, that even people in other religions can sometimes perform an exorcism. This, of course, will not be done in the Name of Jesus. These exorcisms typically only aggravate the problem, but when it does work, the efficacy flows from what he says is a mutual authority that we have over each other on a natural level.[21] We see this clearly to be a practice of the Jews, who, as Our Lord states, were at times effective in casting out demons. Fr. Fortea adds that, for those who believe in Christ but are separated from the Church, faith in Christ and belief in the power of the Name of Jesus are sufficient for exorcisms to work. God, he says, as in Baptism, which requires simply the proper form and matter, does not place "too many conditions on the most essential Christian practices for them to be valid." Thus, even those Christians who do not have valid holy orders or access to priests, are still capable of casting out the devil to a certain extent.[22]

With that in mind, we must tread carefully in praying deliverance prayers and doing binding prayers outside of our authority. If we challenge a demon imprudently, they are permitted to retaliate. Some saints, like St. Benedict, who was not a priest, were able to cast out demons with great efficacy. They had been given a certain powerful gift from the Holy Spirit, which was the decision of God Himself, and not something we can simply lay claim to because we desire it. St.

---

[19] Parents can say something like, "In the Name of Jesus, I bind any demon who is keeping my child together with _____."

[20] Ripperger #7

[21] Ripperger #4

[22] Fortea, 103

Benedict had also reached a particular height of holiness to which most people will not be called, and which made his prayers extremely effective. Never, though, cease praying for someone out of fear of the devil getting mad at you. Be prudent, persevere, and be ready for the battle.

Compendium VII

+ The Church possesses both power and authority over the diabolical. This power over demons can increase based on the holiness of the individual priest.
+ Demons know who has authority and who does not. Only those with proper authority should proceed with an exorcism or use the name of a demon.
+ Authority also exists within the family structure. The father of the family may bless all the members of the family. The father and mother may do binding prayers over each other and their children.
+ There are demons that specifically target the family, so it is important that the father, and the whole family, stay devoted to Our Lord and in a state of grace.
+ Exorcisms, binding prayers, and deliverance prayers are all part of the rich heritage of the Catholic Faith, though few people today are properly aware of them.
+ The binding prayer is an essential tool that all the faithful can use to protect themselves against the ordinary attacks of the Enemy.

Chapter Eight

Sin and the Influence of Satan

When we sin, we participate in the submission to the devil to which Adam and Eve were first subjected. Our sins are acts of cooperation with the plans which guide the Kingdom of Satan. As a result, the demons gain an increased authority over us, particularly if our sins are mortal.

Pope Leo XIII, in his encyclical against Freemasonry, begins with a powerful statement on this reality. He says,

> "The race of man, after its miserable fall from God, the Creator and the Giver of heavenly gifts, 'through the envy of the devil,' separated into two diverse and opposite parts, of which the one steadfastly contends for truth and virtue, the other of those things which are contrary to virtue and to truth. The one is the kingdom of God on earth, namely, the true Church of Jesus Christ; and those who desire from their heart to be united with it, so as to gain salvation, must of necessity serve God and His only-begotten Son with their whole mind and with an entire will. The other is the kingdom of Satan, in whose possession and control are all whosoever follow the fatal example of their leader and of our first parents, those who refuse to obey the divine and eternal law, and who have many aims of their own in contempt of God, and many aims also against God."[1]

When we sin, and when we "follow the fatal example" of Satan and Adam and Eve, and when we disobey the divine and eternal law,

---

[1] Pope Leo XIII, *Humanum Genus*, 1

we fall under the "possession and control" of the Kingdom of Satan. We should all let that sink in. In this era, characterized, as Pope Pius XII said, by a loss of the sense of sin, Satan is more empowered. As Fr. Amorth adds, this quality of our era "helps Satan to act nearly undisturbed and, inducing man to sin, takes man progressively away from the love of God."[2]

In this country, Fr. Ripperger estimates that twenty-five percent of people are diabolically obsessed.[3] There are far too many people opening doors to the demonic through mortal sin. In his talks, he strongly emphasizes that the proper effect of every single mortal sin is possession.[4] The only reason that we do not become possessed when we sin mortally is because God blocks the demon, at least in about ninety-nine percent of cases.[5] When we are in a state of grace, we are subject to God. When we are in a state of sin, we place ourselves under Satan. Our sins, since they are acts in service of the Kingdom of Satan, empower the demons against us.

Gateway Sins

Exorcists refer to these sins as the doorways or gateways by which the demons enter the body of the person. In 416, Pope Innocent I acknowledged that a baptized person can become possessed by the devil as a result of a vice or a sin.[6] St. Alphonsus Liguori describes this reality by saying, "Through the very door, by which God leaves the soul, the devil enters."[7] Fr. Fortea adds that God permits diabolical possession in order to, among other reasons, "punish sinners who seek a relationship with evil."[8]

Gateways for diabolical influence include what are called "vices contrary to nature," such as homosexuality, which is the sin of Sodom. Fr. Ripperger says that if a certain demon is present in a possession, the exorcist knows that there has been sodomitic behavior

---

[2] Amorth, 64
[3] Ripperger #6
[4] See note on page 43.
[5] Ripperger #1
[6] Fortea, 98
[7] *Preparation for Death*, 159
[8] Fortea, 85

in the life of the possessed person.[9] There is a demon related to same-sex attraction for men, Asmodeus, and two for women, Lilith and Leviathan. While in 99.9% of cases of same-sex attraction, the cause of its emergence is some sort of trauma, these demons can cause it without any trauma, by disturbing the intellect and stirring the passions.[10]

Mortal sins occurring in our thoughts can also be gateways to possession. Pride is a good example. Fr. Ripperger told the story of a woman who was tempted through pride to think that she was better than everyone else. After she consented to this thought, she became possessed.[11] St. Alphonsus recounts the story of Jeroboam, connecting sin and vice to obedience to the devil:

> "When Jeroboam rebelled against the Lord, he endeavored to draw the people with him into idolatry. Hence he placed before them his idols, saying, 'Behold thy gods, O Israel.'[12] It is thus the devil acts; he represents a certain pleasure to the sinner, and says, 'Make this your god; behold this pleasure; this revenge is your god; adhere to them, and forsake the Lord.' And in consenting to sin, the sinner obeys the devil, and in his heart adores as his god the pleasure which he indulges. 'A vice in the heart is an idol on the altar'."[13]

When we do our own wills through pride, our wills become devils. The devil does not bother us as much at that point because our wills are willing evil on their own.[14] St. Louis de Montfort adds that, through "the unwholesome presence of self-love, inordinate self-reliance, and self-will," all the many riches and gifts you have received from God will be spoiled.[15]

As previously mentioned, sins committed by family members, in particular the father, can bring demons into homes and into family lines. These generational spirits can cause problems on many levels,

---

[9] Ripperger #2
[10] Ripperger #6, based on his observations and conversations with other exorcists.
[11] Ripperger #2
[12] I Kings 12:28
[13] *Preparation*, 157
[14] *True Spouse of Christ*, 143-144
[15] *True Devotion*, 178

from a general increase of temptations, in their frequency and intensity, to the possession of family members. Fr. Amorth states that he has some uncertainties about generational spirits but adds that he has had a sufficient number of experiences that seem to coalesce into evidence for this reality. Demonic possession cases have, for example, emerged where ancestors of the possessed were involved in witchcraft. He has concluded that a curse "can be transmitted from one generation to the next particularly if it is issued by a father or a mother against a son, his marriage, or his future children."[16]

Possession of Children

Possessions originating from generational spirits can even include children. Some exorcists do not believe children can become possessed, but many exorcists testify to the reality as they have seen it. Fr. Ripperger told the story of a family whose ten-month-old child was thought to be possessed. He held the child himself and the demon manifested and the child tried to gouge out his eyes. They later discovered that it was a generational spirit that had possessed him.[17] As Fr. Amorth puts it, "It may shock some that even a newborn or a young baby can be possessed by a demon, but it is the pure (and terrible) reality with which we exorcists must often deal."[18]

The sources for child possession can be a generational spirit or the involvement of the child, in some way, in a Satanic ritual. Satanists take advantage of the existence of generational spirits and intentionally go about the work necessary to keep a demon within their family line. Fr. Ripperger says that some Satanists have successfully kept the same demon in the family for four hundred years. From the moment the child is in the womb to the moment he is born, they are performing all the commanded rituals in order to ensure the possession of the child.[19] Fr. Amorth refers to the famous case of Francesco Vaiasuso whose possession, which manifested later in life,

---

[16] Amorth, 60
[17] Ripperger #8
[18] Amorth, 79
[19] Ripperger #8

was linked to a satanic ritual that he was forced to be involved in at the age of four.[20]

This dedication of the child to Satan is a "sort of false version of Baptism, but it could very well have a catastrophic effect on that child," says Fr. Grob.[21] The child is vulnerable to the demon, even in the womb, which is why it is possible for parents to do this. Fr. Thomas tells the story of a man who was cursed by his father while the man was still in the womb and suffered sexual abuse when he was two years old. All of his life, until he was thirty-five, he sensed a presence in his life, but mistook it for his guardian angel. Though throughout his life he had been a practicing Catholic, it was only at the age of thirty-five, when he attended an Easter Vigil Mass where a bishop was in attendance, that the demon manifested.[22]

The lack of involvement of the will in the possession of the person in these cases makes the liberation less difficult. When the person is Baptized, the exorcisms that are involved in the rite of Baptism bring a liberation from any evils that might be within or upon the child, such as those from Satanic dedications or generational spirits.[23] The case of the man mentioned above by Fr. Thomas was more complicated due to the abuse that he suffered in addition to the curse in the womb. To demonstrate this power of Baptism, we can look to a vision of St. Mary d'Oignies who "saw a devil go out from an infant who was receiving baptism, and the Holy Ghost enter with a multitude of angels."[24]

Generational Spirits

Fr. Ripperger says that virtually every family has a generational spirit of some sort, which can manifest in many forms. A common source of that spirit, in this era, is likely to be the result of the Freemasonic curse, taken by high-ranking Freemasons, which invokes a generational curse on the entire family line going forward.[25] If there

---

[20] Amorth, 80
[21] Fr. Grob article
[22] Fr. Thomas #2
[23] Fr. Grob article
[24] *Preparation for Death*, 195
[25] Ripperger #6

is a Freemason in the family, who reached any degree at all, not just the highest degree, Father recommends that the people in the family address the potential presence of this curse.[26] This curse leads to the presence of a demon with very distinct patterns of behavior. They typically affect the health of the family, particularly by way of respiratory problems, and tempt the family to sins against the Sixth Commandment, like molestation.[27]

Women come to see exorcists a lot more than men do. This is true for several reasons. Fr. Ripperger says that this is due in part to the devil's hatred for the Blessed Virgin Mary. By extension, the devil hates women. The demons attack women because they know they can get into the family through the woman, as Satan did with Eve.[28] Women are also often victims of abuse, which places them in a spiritually vulnerable state of which the demons will take advantage.[29] Abuse can be a doorway for generational spirits to enter and Satanic groups often use this as part of their rituals. Sexual deviancy is always present in Satanic cults.[30] Women also turn to exorcists more often in part because they are more inclined to turn to the Church in times of need.[31]

Adopted children can also sometimes have a generational spirit. If there are concerns about the behavior being outside of what is normal for a child, it is possible that it could have come from the biological parents.[32] This is exactly why the Church has exorcisms for children in the traditional Rite of Baptism.[33] Sacred Scripture gives a perfect example:

> And they brought the boy to him; and when the spirit saw him, immediately it convulsed the boy, and he fell on the

---

[26] Fr. Ripperger provides a prayer to break the Freemasonic Curse on his website *Sensus Traditionis* – visit http://www.sensustraditionis.org/Freemasonic.pdf

[27] Ripperger #8

[28] Amorth, 81

[29] Ripperger #1

[30] Fr. Thomas #2

[31] Amorth, 81

[32] Ripperger #8

[33] The modern Rite of Baptism does not have the same number, or intensity, of exorcisms present in the Rite that was used in the Church up until its reform in 1999. The old Rite still remains an option for exorcists, most of whom prefer it to the new.

ground and rolled about, foaming at the mouth. And Jesus asked his father, "How long has he had this?" And he said, "From childhood."[34]

Looking at this passage, we see that the father brings his son to Our Lord. When the father is asked how long the demon has been in the boy, the father responds that it has been there from childhood or, in the Latin, from infancy. Thus, this is either from a generational spirit or from a curse, both of which can be addressed by the exorcism at Baptism.

When it comes to ridding your family of the presence of a generational spirit, it is important to remember that God has permitted the demon to be there. The demon is a disturber and a menace but is powerless before God. Therefore, when we turn to God, the demon can be removed. A critical step is to go to Confession. All exorcists say that Confession is more effective than an exorcism. Confession remedies our spiritual lives on multiple levels, all of which make us less inviting to demons. The demons are rendered unable to hold the guilt of our sins against us, the soul becomes radiant with sanctifying grace, our disordered passions are partially corrected, our hatred for sin is increased, and we are supernaturally drawn to think of God due to an increase in the theological virtues.

Fr. Ripperger recommends that we pray to Our Lady specifically under the title "Our Lady of Sorrows."[35] When she was with Simeon at the Presentation of Our Lord in the Temple,[36] and he prophesied that a sword would pierce her soul, she embraced this destiny to suffer with her Son. Her willing suffering with Christ merited an intimacy with God by which she knows things that no one else knows because God reveals them to her. This is the meaning of the verse, "And thy own soul a sword shall pierce, that, out of many hearts, thoughts may be revealed." Our Lady of Sorrows, Father says, will help us detect the demons in our lives and show us how to remove them.[37]

St. Louis de Montfort has two poignant statements that tie in to the reality of generational spirits and the power of Our Lady to assist

---

[34] Mark 9:20-21
[35] See page 149 for more details on Our Lady of Sorrows.
[36] Luke 2:22ff
[37] Ripperger #9

us in removing them. He says, "By obeying the serpent, Eve ruined her children as well as herself and delivered them up to [Satan]. Mary by her perfect fidelity to God saved her children with herself and consecrated them to his divine majesty."[38]   He adds, "She will unmask his serpent's cunning and expose his wicked plots. She will scatter to the winds his devilish plans and to the end of time will keep her faithful servants safe from his cruel claws."[39]

---

[38] *True Devotion*, 53
[39] *True Devotion*, 54

Compendium VIII

+ Mortal sin cuts us off from God's grace and aligns us with the workings of Satan, making us vulnerable to diabolical influences, including possession.
+ In almost all cases of mortal sin, God blocks the demons from proceeding with possession.
+ These sins are referred to as gateway sins, which can open us individually to demons as well as make those in our family more vulnerable to their presence and influence.
+ It is possible for children to be possessed as a result of demons in the family line or through forced involvement of the child in Satanic rituals.
+ One of the powers and purposes of Baptism is to break and remove the presence of any demons in the child.
+ Invoking the aid of the Blessed Virgin Mary under the title "Our Lady of Sorrows" is particularly helpful in detecting and removing demons from our lives.

Chapter Nine

Resisting Diabolical Influence

Fr. Ripperger says that demons have a core principle which guides them: "Anything but God!" So, we must keep our focus on God, and they will leave us alone.

In these times, which try the most faithful of souls, and lure the many to veer from the right path, chasing after the wonders of the modern age, with abundant moral and technological novelties, those souls which yearn for strength and protection from evil often do not know where to find it. They have a basic understanding of the tradition of prayer and recourse to the Sacraments to which the Church calls them, but the many powerful weapons which Our Lord has entrusted to His Church throughout the ages have, to a great extent, been forgotten.

Priests, teachers, and lay theologians today are engaged in what might be called 'spiritual archaeology,' digging into the past to unearth what has become hidden beneath the collapse of Christian culture. Exorcists like Fr. Ripperger, Fr. Amorth, Fr. Fortea, Fr. Thomas, and the other exorcists mentioned in this book, and all the devout and faithful priests and teachers of the Faith, who hand on the sacred traditions, present them to us with hands metaphorically stained with mud and dirt. When we behold what they offer, we often say, "I've never heard that before." However, we must let that statement spring from faith and not from doubt and see that these spiritual relics are authentic and not simply something that they conceived of themselves.

This introduction is necessary as we reflect on the means which the Church has given to us so that we may be fortified and prepared for battle. Sacramentals and traditional spiritual practices will strengthen us as temples where the Holy Spirit resides; they will sharpen our spiritual warfare tactics for this combat in which we have been enlisted by our Baptism.

St. Louis de Montfort provides us with an important reflection on the importance of the vow we all make at our Baptism. He recalls what St. Thomas said, that "men vow in Baptism to renounce the devil and all his seductions." This vow, he continues, according to St. Augustine, "is the greatest and the most indispensable of all vows."[1] The Catechism of the Council of Trent calls upon the faithful to take up the practice of renewing our baptismal promises more frequently in order to combat the grave disorders in the Christian life. This Catechism states, "The parish priest shall exhort the faithful never to lose sight of the fact that they are bound in conscience to dedicate and consecrate themselves for ever to their Lord and Redeemer as his slaves."[2] Fr. Amorth says that reciting the Creed, and the renunciations of Satan from the renewal of Baptismal promises, "serves to break off every tie with the Evil One," particularly for those who have had experience with the occult.[3]

As we begin laying out the means for properly resisting diabolical influences, let us briefly revisit some fundamental concepts related to the issue of diabolical possession. As Fr. Ripperger has said, there are three ways that one may get possessed.[4] The first is through mortal sin. This is the one that must be remembered at all times, and which this chapter will address in great detail. The proper effect of every mortal sin, though typically blocked by God, is possession. This includes all mortal sins, such as pride, fornication, and pornography, among others. However, God is completely in control of the activity of the demons and He alone can permit the possession to occur. Mortal sin opens the door for them to enter the soul, but they may not enter unless Christ permits them. As Fr. Ripperger has said, in all but the rarest cases God blocks them.

When a possession does occur, there are typically signs indicating the demon is present. One of the many signs previously discussed will appear in the person's life. Fr. Weber, when he was training to become an exorcist, was advised to "look for a sudden hostility toward God and religion and holy things that did not exist before." This

---

[1] *True Devotion*, 127
[2] *True Devotion*, 128-9
[3] Amorth, 23
[4] Ripperger #2

would be an indicator of a potential possession.[5] Fr. Ripperger says that demons are showy and like to show off once they have accomplished something, so there will be a change in the person if possession occurs.[6]

However, if a person has committed a mortal sin and there is no change noticed, then there should be no worry about possession. Pray, get to Confession, do penance, "go, and sin no more."[7] If you notice something that is clearly diabolical, then speak to a good priest about it. If you do not notice anything, then it is best to take your mind off of that worry and keep it focused on God. Even if there is a demon present, you've taken the first step in casting it back out.

The second way a person can become possessed is when people have undergone some kind of trauma, like rape or abuse. Witnessing something traumatic, or personally suffering an abuse, can cause a deep wound that needs to be healed. Without that healing, it can open us up to negative emotions and thoughts.[8] When a person acts in an evil manner upon another person or a thing, through abuse or some sort of traumatic attack, they act in a disordered way upon them, and the devil can get a hold on the person or thing at that point.[9] Fr. Martins said that trauma "can lead to losing faith in the goodness of God and the world He created." Trauma, he says, can "leave a wound and that wound can shake us in the goodness of reality."[10] He adds that a spirit of fear can latch on to a person as a result.

Fr. Thomas says that eighty percent of people who come to see him are victims of abuse.[11] He adds that the wound from abuse tends to gain a diabolical component when the victim, in order to find healing or peace, becomes open to and dabbles in the occult. The abuse becomes a doorway making invitations to evil more easily accepted.[12] Fr. Amorth, speaking about the negative power of abuse, says that the

---

[5] Fr. Weber video
[6] Ripperger #2
[7] John 8:11
[8] Fr. Grob video
[9] Ripperger #2
[10] Fr. Martins video
[11] Fr. Thomas #2
[12] Fr. Thomas #1

female victim of a Satanic "Black Mass" often suffers the consequence of the ritual, which is possession.[13]

To illustrate the power of the demonic to attach itself to things that are used in evil ways, Fr. Ripperger told the story of an exorcist who visited a house where strange things were reported to be happening. The former owner of the house had shot and killed his wife in the backyard. When the priest visited the home, he was looking around and found a shotgun shell in the area where the murder occurred. Father says that "from the moment he picked it up to the moment he destroyed it, everything in his life went wrong."[14] Fr. Fortea comments on the importance of handling such objects. In some exorcisms, a cursed object is vomited up by the possessed. If this happens, the exorcist must not touch the item, and must burn it, not throw it away. If he does handle the object, "he should continue praying while doing so. His hands must be washed with holy water. If not, these types of objects may cause him health problems for some time."[15]

The third way to become possessed is extremely rare: purely by the will of God. One of the few examples of this, Fr. Ripperger says, involved a nun in Iowa. The exorcist commanded the demon inside of her to reveal the sin that she had committed which led to the possession. The demon admitted that the nun had committed no such sin. The demon went on to say that there was a sin in the region and God desired that reparation be made for that sin. As a result of that information, they set up perpetual adoration throughout the diocese and, in three days, she was liberated from the demon.[16]

God permits the possession of someone in a state of grace, through a spell, for example, because, according to Fr. Fortea, "many times the evils that occur to a person's body in a possession are a source of blessings for the soul."[17] One woman, for example, whom Fr. Ripperger knew, and who was possessed, achieved a great degree

---

[13] Amorth, 37

[14] Ripperger #2

[15] Fortea, 110

[16] Ripperger #2

[17] Fortea, 83

of holiness through her battle against the demon, to the point where she appeared to be basically sinless.[18]

As was just demonstrated, possession can only occur if we choose to commit a mortal sin, if we are the victims of, or associated with, an event of great trauma, or if God, in a unique and rare permission, simply allows the possession to occur. As a result, we have nothing to fear if we stay close to Our Lord. The devil is active, but he is not behind every door or ready to pounce whenever we sin. Fidelity to Christ and recourse to the aids He gives us in the Sacraments and sacramentals is sufficient to protect us. At that point, if God did permit a demon to enter your life, you would know how to respond. Here, recall the words of St. Peter,

> "Humble yourselves therefore under the mighty hand of God, that in due time he may exalt you. Cast all your anxieties on him, for he cares about you. Be sober, be watchful. Your adversary the devil prowls around like a roaring lion, seeking some one to devour. Resist him, firm in your faith."[19]

Adding to this emphasis on faith, St. John of the Cross speaks about the powerlessness experienced by the devil when he confronts a soul who is strong in this virtue. He says,

> "When the soul journeys in its vestment of faith, the devil can neither see it nor succeed in harming it, since it is well protected by faith – more so than by all the other virtues – against the devil, who is at once the strongest and the most cunning of enemies. It is clear that Saint Peter could find no better protection than faith to save him from the devil, when he said: *Cui resistite fortes in fide.*[20] And in order to gain the grace of the Beloved, and union with Him, the soul cannot put on a better vest and tunic, to serve as a foundation and beginning of the other vestments of the virtues, than this white garment of faith, for without it, as the Apostle says, it is

---

[18] Ripperger #2
[19] I Peter 5:6-9
[20] "Resist him, firm in your faith."

impossible to please God, and with it, it is impossible to fail to please Him."[21]

Here is an image for the devil which might drive home many points to be remembered. The devil, with all of his demons, is like a charlatan, a trickster, or a circus. We must not let him lure us to his performance for, while he has wonders to show us and great tricks to perform to amuse us, he also has lions and other wild things set to devour us, and he captures souls to transform into freaks of nature. The strangeness, novelty, and danger of the devil draws many to take a look and see what he is all about. At that point, they appear in his vision and he becomes invested in pulling them in completely. However, if we resist him and ignore him, denying his advertisements and enticements, he will pack up his performance and go somewhere else.

Remember, though, he comes uninvited, and he can return uninvited as well. As Our Lord indicates about the devil,[22] if he is driven away, he returns with greater strength and dedication to the mission of destruction. As a result, we must be vigilant: know where he travels, know what entices him, know his associates, know what he despises, and act accordingly.

Ignore the Devil

The devil and the demons, though they prefer to go unnoticed, also crave attention and glory, so the best course is to ignore them. Ignore them first and primarily by loving God and staying in a state of grace. Ignore them second by dismissing their suggestions and ignoring their presence. There is a famous story of St. Teresa of Avila that demonstrates this approach. She was lying in bed and sensed a spiritual presence above her. Fearing it was God, she rolled over to see who it was. Instead of God, it was the devil who had manifested above her bed. In response, she simply said, "Oh, it's just you," and she rolled over and went to sleep.

---

[21] *Dark Night of the Soul*, 119
[22] cf. Matt 12:45

The best thing to do is to treat the demons like bad thoughts: ignore them and take your mind off of them. Fr. Ripperger advises that, if you see something strange and think that it might be demonic, simply pray and move on. If it continues or becomes stranger, then get a priest involved. Also, do not first think that it is from the devil, but look for a natural explanation.[23] Fr. Fortea says that, "Given the nature of demonic temptation, the best remedy is to pray and ignore the temptation as much as possible and do exactly the opposite of what is proposed."[24]

If the demon is not complying at some point in an exorcism, Fr. Ripperger says he just ignores them. The demons find this to be irritating since they want their resistance to be acknowledged and want the priest to get irritated themselves. This is the opposite of what Eve did, who failed to ignore the devil, which the demons took delight in. It irritates them when we do not go along.[25]

St. John of the Cross gives us clear counsel about how to react to strange phenomena, even if we think it might be coming from God: ignore it.[26] Fr. Antonio Moreno, in an article on St. John of the Cross, says, though extraordinary phenomena "are sometimes from God, they are more often from the devil."[27] To ignore these things is a prudent course to take. Prudence is a virtue and we never offend God by being virtuous. Curiosity can be a vice, though, and the devil has lured many souls to himself, beginning with Eve, through this sin. In this context of curiosity for signs, Fr. Ripperger warns against getting caught up in the Charismatic movement which, as he points out, is a "signs and wonders movement."[28]

During the course of an exorcism, this counsel is very important for exorcists to follow as well. The various manifestations of the demon are in part employed to distract the priest. Demons know the weaknesses of the priest and will try to 'push the right button' to destabilize him. The demon is also playing with the priest's mind in the process, trying to take his focus off of the exorcism, push him to in-

---

[23] Ripperger #1
[24] Fortea, 49
[25] Ripperger #7
[26] Ripperger #4
[27] https://www.catholicculture.org/culture/library/view.cfm?recnum=8280
[28] Ripperger #4

ternal deliberations, and, there, in his mind, drive him to sin. One tactic of the demon is to bring up the sins of the priest, and his flaws and weaknesses, which the demon would know.[29] Pushing those buttons, the demon tries to undermine the priest's faith, hope, and charity, leading him to doubt God's power and mercy, and slowly weakening him such that he is incapable, or unwilling, to perform the exorcism properly.

Fr. Ripperger told a story about an exorcism where the local Bishop had taken part, though not as the primary exorcist. During the course of the exorcism, the demon stopped talking to the exorcist and called out the Bishop for a sin that he had very recently committed. What the demon said turned out to be true.[30] Fr. Grob says that the demons are able to bring up sins which have not been confessed. "Sin is the domain of darkness," he says, and "when sin is confessed it is covered with the Precious Blood of Jesus, it's removed. But the Evil One watches and observes. He sees our habits. He sees our practices. He sees what we do."[31]

Mental Stability

Sin causes damage to us in every way: physically, intellectually, and in the power of our will. Sin can damage and kill our bodies. Sin can train us to think that evil is good and good is evil. Sin can train us to love and desire evil, and to detest and avoid good. Sin wounds us, and these wounds can come to us through our own sins and through the sins of other people. St. Louis de Montfort says that "the actual sins we have committed, whether mortal or venial, even though forgiven, have intensified our base desires, our weakness, our inconstancy and our evil tendencies, and have left a sediment of evil in our soul."[32] These weaknesses and wounds become the focal points of the devil's temptations.[33]

Some demons are referred to as "clinging spirits," which attach to our wounds and seek to prevent the healing that they require. These

---

[29] Ripperger #1
[30] Ripperger #2
[31] Fr. Grob video
[32] *True Devotion*, 79
[33] Amorth, 64

spirits can also attach themselves to the wounds that have come through sinful sexual contact or emotionally abusive relationships. In addition to being a grave sin, these behaviors have also created deep but unhealthy bonds to people. After these have been brought to Confession, and "although our sin is forgiven, the demons want to prevent deep emotional and spiritual healing."[34]

Grudges and grievances and refusals to forgive others can prevent exorcisms from progressing as they should. As Fr. Ripperger points out, "everyone in heaven has forgiven everyone, but the opposite is the case in Hell."[35] If we hang on to hatred, we make the demons feel at home, and they will not want to leave as easily.

Self-knowledge is vital to spiritual health. This requires faith, to beseech God to enlighten you, and humility, to fully accept what He reveals about yourself. Self-deception is an easy thing to slip into, and it is something of which the devil can take advantage. We are also able, through the presence of vice in the soul, to truly believe that something which is evil is actually good and harmless, where the opposite is very much the case. This knowledge extends to our memories, which may linger in our mind to a greater or lesser extent. Fr. Ripperger recommends praying for forgetfulness and purification of the memory. Demons can use these memories to influence our imagination, which will influence our emotions and inclinations, which can be a set up for sin.[36] This forgetfulness can also help bring about the healing of old wounds, which are a focal point of the devil's activity in our lives.

---

[34] Fortea, 95
[35] Ripperger #6
[36] Ripperger #3

Compendium IX

+ There are many sacred traditions in our Faith of which people are, more or less, unaware today but which exorcists see and teach to be valuable sources of spiritual strength.

+ There are three ways by which a person may become possessed, each depending on God's permission: mortal sin, serious trauma, and by the will of God.

+ Demons attach themselves to people, things, and places when disorder is introduced. This includes abuse and trauma. These are grave wounds which the demons seek to exploit.

+ Faith and a serious focus on God are sufficient to protect us against possession and serious diabolical influence.

+ In every way, it is best to ignore the devil, whether in ordinary temptation or extraordinary manifestations. If something continues or becomes more serious, then get a priest involved.

+ Sin and vices damage us and create wounds, which are burdens that destabilize us and make us more vulnerable to diabolical influences.

+ It is important to be honest about our weaknesses and to seek the healing of our past and our vices in order to proceed more steadily in the spiritual life.

Chapter Ten

Protecting Your Spiritual Life

God, says Origen, is more solicitous for our salvation, than the devil is for our perdition; for the Lord loves our souls far more than the devil hates them.[1]

These words, conveyed to us in the writings of St. Alphonsus Liguori, point us to the abundant means which Our Lord has given us through His Church, by which we may the more securely attain our salvation. These means are weapons in a spiritual battle in which we were recruited at our Baptism. "Christians," as Pope Leo XIII strongly affirms, "are born for combat."[2] The more mightily we fight, the more assuredly will we triumph. Hear, too, another admonition of St. Alphonsus on this point, when he says, "Remember that now more than ever you must prepare yourself for conflicts, because your enemies, the world, the devil, and the flesh, will arm themselves now more than ever to fight against you in order to deprive you of all that you have acquired."[3] Thus, we must protect the great treasures of grace which Our Lord has so generously bestowed upon us.

Fr. Ripperger says that, when God bestows sanctifying grace upon someone, He protects this grace with actual graces.[4] He sees it as something from which He guarantees, and expects, a return. This is clear from the Parable of the Talents.[5] As a result, He seeks to secure the grace He imparts, that it would not return without bearing fruit. Isaiah describes the Word of God in a similar manner:

"And as the rain and the snow come down from heaven, and return no more thither, but soak the earth, and water it, and

---

[1] *Preparation for Death*, 99
[2] Pope Leo XIII, *Sapientiae Christianae* 14
[3] *Preparation*, 312
[4] Ripperger #7
[5] Matthew 25:14-30

make it to spring, and give seed to the sower, and bread to the eater: So shall my word be, which shall go forth from my mouth: it shall not return to me void, but it shall do whatsoever I please, and shall prosper in the things for which I sent it."[6]

The Word of God is Our Lord and the grace He bestows is His own divine life. Therefore, what He has bestowed on us shall not return to Him void, but "shall prosper in the things for which [He] sent it," thus fulfilling His will.

As long as we remain in a state of grace, we will be protected by Our Lord. This is His promise. He says, "If a man loves me, he will keep my word, and my Father will love him, and we will come to him and make our home with him."[7] With the Blessed Trinity dwelling within us, nothing can disturb us. This is what St. Teresa of Avila is conveying in her famous prayer:

> Let nothing disturb you,
> Let nothing frighten you,
> All things are passing:
> God never changes.
> Patience obtains all things.
> Whoever has God lacks nothing;
> God alone suffices.

The critical work, then, is to remain in a state of grace and under God's protection, that we may always live in this place of peace. When we step out from under God's protection, we are no longer protected but have then exposed ourselves to many dangers. We must be serious in our dedication to obedience to Christ. Half-heartedness can lead to living a life with good intentions but a lack of follow-through. "Good intentions," as Fr. Fortea puts it, "are worth nothing; the law of God is objective and must be obeyed."[8]

---

[6] Isaiah 55:10-11 DR
[7] John 14:23
[8] Fortea, 108

Demons are predators, as Fr. Ripperger explains.[9] They prowl around looking for the weakest and easiest prey. As when a cheetah hunts a gazelle, it takes down the one it can most easily acquire, which is usually the slowest or the one in closest proximity to its danger, so too does a demon pursue those who are closest on its own course. These are the spiritually wounded and spiritually limping, who are ignorant of the medicine that the Church provides or are seeking truth outside of Christ. As Fr. Thomas puts it, when someone opens themselves up to seeking answers through the occult, "an entity may come because it smells blood."[10]

In order to avoid this predatory behavior, one of the things we must do is allow Our Lord to heal us. These wounds and weaknesses can and must be healed by the grace of Our Lord Jesus Christ flowing through His Church. When Our Lord permitted Himself to be killed, He did so in fulfillment of the prophecy of Isaiah which said, "by His stripes we are healed."[11] Thus, it is the suffering and wounding of Christ that accomplished our healing and salvation. The wounds by which He shed His Precious Blood merited for us a full and complete healing: physically, psychologically, spiritually, and morally. St. Gregory Nazianzus said, "What has not been assumed has not been healed." Our Lord assumed our entire human nature. Therefore, it is possible for us to come to a total and complete healing through Him.

When this healing comes about, it will literally block the demons from latching on to us. The healing will necessarily come about as a result of an increase of faith and devotion to Our Lord. This is the course that many of the great saints have taken, who went about seeking to heal and conquer the disordered passions of their flesh. After this victory, they became the great enemies of the devil which we know them to be.

Fr. Amorth says, "The demon keeps his distance from the one who nurtures his faith, who frequents the sacraments, and who wishes to live devoutly."[12] This rise in holiness, which a reliance on Christ will bring, will increase the efficacy of our spiritual warfare efforts. The Fathers of the Church frequently mentioned, in the first three cen-

---

[9] Ripperger #7
[10] Fr. Thomas #2
[11] Isaiah 53:5
[12] Amorth, 21

turies of the Church, that the disciples had the power to cast out demons. A great number of these were monks, like St. Benedict, whose efficacy against evil flowed from their asceticism and holiness.[13] According to the rules of the Church at that time, exorcisms were not yet restricted to priests working with the authority of the Bishop.

General Means of Protection

Now, let us turn to the abundant advice that priests and exorcists give in order to protect our spiritual lives and make easier progress along the path to salvation. An important note here, as was mentioned before, is that these priests and exorcists are steeped in the traditions of the Church and have done the spiritual work necessary to uncover the ancient riches of the Faith that have become obscure to us in this current age of the Church. As a result, some of the things they advise will seem foreign to us, or we may think they are old superstitions that were condemned by the modern Church. Nevertheless, they are authentically Catholic.

I have processed these thoughts myself. Having returned to the Faith almost twenty years ago, I have been in a never-ending process of learning the truths of the Faith from wise and learned priests. We must be careful how we develop our beliefs, and cling always to the holy Bride of Christ, and thus stay fully attached to the Vine, which is Christ. This is an effort that has always been present in the life of Christians. Even in the apostolic age, these warnings were given, as seen in St. Paul's admonition to Timothy:

> I charge you in the presence of God and of Christ Jesus who is to judge the living and the dead, and by his appearing and his kingdom: preach the word, be urgent in season and out of season, convince, rebuke, and exhort, be unfailing in patience and in teaching. For the time is coming when people will not endure sound teaching, but having itching ears they will accumulate for themselves teachers to suit their own likings, and will turn away from listening to the truth and wander into

---

[13] Amorth, 98

myths. As for you, always be steady, endure suffering, do the work of an evangelist, fulfil your ministry.[14]

It is the work of every Catholic to discern well so as not to follow after those teachers who have been hired to teach a doctrine of myths and fables, forgetful of the truths handed down by Our Lord and His Apostles.

Exorcists are very understanding and empathetic toward people who are dealing with diabolical influences. They know that people are suffering intensely with these problems and their eagerness to help is amplified by this compassion. They are also very focused when they offer advice and counsel. Exorcists take a lot of time with a person who comes to see them in order to properly diagnose, not just whether it is a medical or spiritual problem, but what is the exact nature of the spiritual problem. Demons can enter through one sin, but then stir up the passions and drive a person intensely toward a different sin. Often, the person cannot see which sin is the true problem, but the exorcist can. As a result, the efforts of the exorcist are directed at the most precise spiritual warfare possible.

State of Grace

The first and most critical piece in our spiritual armor, in the effort of resisting diabolical influences, is to be, and remain always, in a state of grace. As Fr. Ripperger puts it, "Never fall into mortal sin ever!"[15] Demons do not like to get involved with us if we are in a state of grace. As was mentioned earlier, God has invested His grace in us and He will protect it. The state of grace also merits protection for us due to our fidelity to His covenant. In that state, Our Lord is very much inclined to grant our petitions for protection. When we leave the state of grace, that protection is not something that He has then promised to give, since we have pushed Him away. Suffering, as a result of sin, is a medicinal punishment that can be used to bring us back and teach us to take sin seriously.

---

[14] 2 Tim 4:1-5
[15] See definition of mortal sin on page 43. Also Ripperger #1

It is critical to lead a good Catholic life. This includes, among many other things, Mass, and weekly or monthly Confession. This will maintain and strengthen the soul in a state of grace. Fr. Fortea says that, when we are in a state of grace, we are an "unpleasant dwelling for a demon."[16] Fr. Amorth says, "The devil is more tranquil if he does not have to live with prayer, fasting, the Eucharist, and the other sacramental practices."[17] If we are living a normal, good Catholic life, the odds of being diabolically influenced are rare, though it can still happen.

Those who separate themselves from the Faith are more exposed to the danger of the devil's activity, as their souls are more welcoming to him.[18] Similarly, when mortal sin is committed in a house, the demons see this as an invitation to take up residence there. This invitation must then be formally rescinded and replaced with the blessings of Almighty God.[19] This is how generational spirits enter families, particularly through the father, but also through any member of the family. Demons target the father as the head of the family, and they target the mother, as they first did with Eve, through whom they can also enter the home.

When Adam chose to eat the forbidden fruit, and listen to Satan, he entered into a relationship with him, and gave over to Satan his own authority. This brought Adam, and all of us, into bondage and slavery to the Evil One. Whenever we move away from God and goodness, we make a bond with evil. These connections give the demons a right to act on us and in our lives.[20]

Liberation from evil, regarding both the presence of demons in our lives, and the inclination to evil in our souls, is the goal of the Christian life. The prayer that Our Lord taught us ends with the line, "Deliver us from evil," which is also translated, "Deliver us from the Evil One." This depth of meaning is important, and both components must be remembered.

---

[16] Fortea, 68
[17] Amorth, 67
[18] Amorth, 67
[19] Fr. Martins video
[20] Fr. Martins video

Fr. Amorth sees the statement of Our Lord, "In my Name, they will cast out demons,"[21] as applying to self-liberation. For this to occur, though, it must be joined to "living a life of grace, approaching the sacraments, invoking the help of Mary and the saints, and praying with faith."[22] Liberation is a gift from God. As Fr. Amorth also says, "In order to liberate oneself, it is necessary to live in the grace of God, to pardon the one who has done evil, to eradicate vices, and to break those human ties that keep him close to the Evil One."[23]

Confession

As part of that life of grace, frequent Confession must be central. Fr. Ripperger says that Confession "is one of the most effective things to ward off or break demonic influence."[24] If a man is trying to conquer a mortal sin, he should go to Confession weekly. If he is trying to avoid mortal sin, he should be going at least once a month.[25] Fr. Amorth adds that Confession, as a Sacrament, is more efficacious than an exorcism, which is only a sacramental.[26] Further, as Fr. Fortea says, "Exorcism only drives out a demon from one's body; confession drives out evil from one's soul."[27] St. Alphonsus Liguori says, regarding Confession, "In the house which is often swept there is no uncleanness."[28] Not only does Confession purify the soul through the remission of sins, but it also gives the helps to resist temptations in the future.

St. Alphonsus relates a story about the eternity of hell in relation to the need for Confession and the intention of reforming one's life. He says,

"In the spiritual exercises of Father Paul Segneri, written by Muratori, it is related that in Rome, a devil in the body of a man possessed, being asked how long he would remain in

---

[21] Mark 16:17
[22] Amorth, 109
[23] Amorth, 87
[24] Ripperger #3
[25] Ripperger #4
[26] Amorth, 87
[27] Fortea, 70
[28] *Preparation for Death*, 322

hell, began to beat his hand against a chair, and answered in a rage, "Forever, forever!" At hearing this great sermon of two words, *forever, forever*, many students of the Roman seminary, who were present, made a general confession, and changed their lives."[29]

Fr. Ripperger recommends paying attention to the sins which may be motivating the sins you confess, as these may be more important than the ones you notice more easily. He also recommends, repeating the teaching of Pope Leo X, to confess the sins of your past life[30] in order to make reparation and to stay out of them in the future. He says, "Exorcists note that confessing the defect, even with that sin, calms it down so it cannot function." He cautioned, too, that many priests may resist your desire to do this, but it truly is a good thing to do.[31]

The Eucharist

In addition to going to Mass on Sundays and Holy Days of Obligation, which are binding under pain of mortal sin, we should also go to Mass as frequently as possible, since the Eucharist truly imparts spiritual strength. The Council of Trent refers to the Eucharist as the medicine which delivers us from venial sins and preserves us from mortal sins.[32] Fr. Fortea says, "Our body is like a home or tent in which He comes to dwell. Nothing destroys demonic influence more powerfully than worthy reception of the Body of Christ."[33]

St. Alphonsus Liguori provides us with several images, from the great saints and Doctors of the Church, which should stir our desire to receive Our Lord in Holy Communion as much as possible. St. Rose of Lima, he says, when she received Our Lord in the Eucharist, felt as if she were receiving the Sun, whose radiance then poured out from her. St. John Chrysostom said that "the Eucharist is a fire which inflames us, that, like lions breathing fire, we may retire from the altar

---

[29] *Preparation for Death*, 280

[30] Previous years of living, of course; not reincarnation.

[31] Ripperger #10

[32] *Preparation for Death*, 323

[33] Fortea, 68

being made terrible to the devil." This fire, St. Alphonsus adds, is a flame of love which inflames the soul so intensely that "breathing such flames of love…the devil shall no longer dare to tempt us."[34]

Finally, let us listen to the wisdom of St. Frances de Sales in his counsel as to why it is important for all to receive Holy Communion frequently:

"If men of the world ask why you communicate so often, tell them that it is that you may learn to love God; that you may be cleansed from imperfections, set free from trouble, comforted in affliction, strengthened in weakness. Tell them that there are two manner of men who need frequent Communion – those who are perfect, since being ready they were much to blame did they not come to the Source and Fountain of all perfection; and the imperfect, that they may learn how to become perfect; the strong, lest they become weak, and the weak, that they may become strong; the sick that they may be healed, and the sound lest they sicken. Tell them that you, imperfect, weak and ailing, need frequently to communicate with your Perfection, your Strength, your Physician. Tell them that those who are but little engaged in worldly affairs should communicate often, because they have leisure; and those who are heavily pressed with business, because they stand so much in need of help; and he who is hard worked needs frequent and substantial food. Tell them that you receive the Blessed Sacrament that you may learn to receive it better; one rarely does that well which one seldom does. Therefore, my child, communicate frequently, – as often as you can, subject to the advice of your spiritual Father. Our mountain hares turn white in winter, because they live in, and feed upon, the snow, and by dint of adoring and feeding upon Beauty, Goodness, and Purity itself in this most Divine Sacrament you too will become lovely, holy, pure."[35]

---

[34] *Preparation for Death*, 358
[35] *Devout Life*, 83

In an exorcism, the priest will sometimes feed the Eucharist to the possessed prior to the start of the rite. Fr. Thomas says that, when he has done this, he has sometimes seen intense reactions from the demon. He says, when he presents the Eucharist to the possessed, "I've had people where they've wanted to launch out the window, because of the power of the Real Presence."[36]

In addition to Confession and the Eucharist, we must receive all of the Sacraments available to us and receive often those which may be repeated. It is also important to receive any Sacrament that you may have missed in the normal course of things. In one exorcism, for example, Fr. Ripperger was helping someone who, it was discovered, had never received Confirmation. The person was then confirmed and there was a drastic reduction in the strength of the demon in the possession.[37]

Humility

"God resisteth the proud, but to the humble he giveth grace."[38]

Demons cannot endure humility.[39] God, on the other hand, favors the humble. We see both of these realities in the life of the Blessed Virgin Mary. The humble man will respond to God's promptings, which enables God to stop the efforts of the demon against the man. The great saints all praise the virtue of humility. It is said that, to St. John Vianney, a man known for his humility, the devil appeared and said, "If there were three such priests as you, my kingdom would be ruined." On the contrary, God is not able to work with the man who is proud, and who thinks that he can do anything he wants, and who has no regard for his limitations and weaknesses. As Fr. Ripperger says, "Pride blocks God's ability to work through us."[40]

---

[36] Fr. Thomas #2
[37] Ripperger #7
[38] 1 Peter 5:5
[39] Lowliness that flows from proper self-knowledge and submission to God's law.
[40] Ripperger #1

Prayer and Meditation

"He who keeps before his eyes the eternal truths – death, judgment, eternity – will not fall into sin."[41]

A regular life of prayer and meditation[42] is both a requirement of justice and a necessary instrument to achieve the strength and stability necessary to avoid and remove demonic influences.[43] We must give God worship as is required by the divine law. This is not an external necessity but corresponds to our spiritual nature. Without a connection to Our Lord, we will die spiritually. In this state of dying, we are easy prey for the demons.

Demons attack us on the level of the intellect, which is where prayer occurs.[44] Fr. Fortea says that, since prayer causes our intellects and wills to be centered on God, it blocks the demons from tempting us. He adds, "Eventually a demon cannot resist this and leaves us alone"[45] Prayer and meditation thus fortify us in this spiritual warfare. Demons do not like to bother with people who pray because prayer makes the person more sensitive and much more likely to recognize their activity. Fr. Ripperger says that, if they dare to take on that kind of person, they will likely end up taking a beating and getting humiliated. He adds, "God may still allow it, but they will not be victorious."[46]

Demons cannot tolerate remaining in a person when they pray. The effects of prayer on the person make them a less suitable dwelling place for the demon. In meditation, God enlightens us, "speaks to us, and makes known to us what we are to avoid, and what we are to do."[47] Prayer calms down the emotions and orders the faculties of the soul so we can better notice and respond to God's promptings. People

---

[41] *Preparation for Death*, 323

[42] Also called mental prayer, is simply defined by St. Teresa of Avila: "Nothing else than an intimate friendship, a frequent heart-to-heart with Him by whom we know ourselves to be loved."

[43] Ripperger #7

[44] Prayer is the lifting up of the mind and heart to God, like faith, which is the supernatural assent of the intellect.

[45] Fortea, 51

[46] Ripperger #7

[47] *Preparation for Death*, 323

who practice daily meditation are able to discern the subtleties of grace and, as Fr. Ripperger says, "can discern if something comes through emotions or through grace."[48] It will eventually break any hold the demon may have on the person, such as with diabolical obsession. The demons are less likely to attack someone who prays, but, as Fr. Ripperger says, demons "cannot stand being defeated, but they are compulsive and want to punish us," so they keep trying.[49]

If there is a diabolical influence in a person's life, prayer can bring that to the surface or drive the demon out completely, depending on the level of diabolical activity.[50] These demons may have been hiding in the person for some time but have gone unnoticed since they were not threatened by grace. A new or renewed prayer life threatens their abode in the person and they either leave or begin to manifest.[51] It is possible that the person only occasionally noticed a disturbance in the past. Fr. Amorth says that sacred places, such as Marian shrines, as well as retreats, processions, and Eucharistic adoration, can be the moment when the person realizes the possession is present. While it is disturbing at that moment, it is, as Fr. Amorth says, truly a gift from God since "only in knowing the illness can one intervene."[52] These sacred places can also bring many liberations from evil spirits simply by being present in that consecrated location. Fr. Amorth related a similar story of St. John Bosco who liberated a girl from a demon simply by walking into the Church dressed in sacred vestments to offer Mass.[53]

Saints and exorcists recommend certain prayers above others due to the efficacy of the devotion. First and foremost is the Rosary. From its beginning, the Rosary has been effective in converting heretics, driving away demons, obtaining miracles, and increasing the sanctity of all who pray it devoutly. Not only is it powerful in these ways, it is the best tool for meditation, and should be prayed daily. St. Alphonsus says that fifteen minutes of prayer a day is sufficient to

---

[48] Ripperger #9
[49] Ripperger #1
[50] Ripperger #7. He says that prayer can end the obsession, but it only brings the possession to the surface.
[51] Fr. Thomas #2
[52] Amorth, 69
[53] Amorth, 22

fulfill the moral obligation to pray every day. One set of mysteries of the Rosary is an ideal way to fulfill this obligation.

Fr. Amorth recommends the Rosary as "an extremely powerful arm against the devil," beneficial to anyone who suffers from a spiritual evil. He says the Rosary has "a strong power of protection and liberation from evil," a power so great, as revealed by Sister Lucia, that "there is no evil that cannot be defeated by its recitation with faith."[54] Fr. Ripperger reminds us that the Rosary was a treasured prayer of Padre Pio. Padre Pio said that the Rosary is the weapon against evil. It will protect the person who prays it faithfully and will help drive out the devil.[55] Fr. Fortea adds, "If a person prays the Rosary daily and asks God to protect him from all the snares of the Evil One, he has nothing to fear."[56]

The saints, in their writings, have emphasized how Our Lady has appeared many times to saints in order to convince them of the power of just one Hail Mary. St. Louis de Montfort, famous for his deep and insightful devotion to Our Lady, says the following about the Hail Mary:

"When the Hail Mary is well said, that is, with attention, devotion and humility, it is, according to the saints, the enemy of Satan, putting him to flight; it is the hammer that crushes him, a source of holiness for souls, a joy to the angels and a sweet melody for the devout."[57]

St. Louis de Montfort also recommends praying the Magnificat of Our Lady.[58] He recounts the writings of another in which it is said that many miracles have been worked through this prayer. He says, "The devils take to flight when they hear these words, 'He puts forth his arm in strength and scatters the proud-hearted'."[59]

---

[54] Amorth, 123
[55] Ripperger #7
[56] Fortea, 25
[57] *True Devotion*, 253
[58] Luke 1:46-55
[59] *True Devotion*, 255

Sacramentals

"Holy Mother Church has, moreover, instituted sacramentals. These are sacred signs which bear a resemblance to the sacraments. They signify effects, particularly of a spiritual nature, which are obtained through the intercession of the Church. By them men are disposed to receive the chief effect of the sacraments, and various occasions in life are rendered holy."[60]

The use of sacramentals in spiritual warfare is highly effective, as they wield, when used, the specific blessing placed on them by Holy Mother Church. The demons discern the presence of this blessing and interact with the sacramental like a soldier against an enemy's weapon. Fr. Thomas says that "we very much underestimate the power of our Sacraments and our sacramentals." He adds that these can be "trigger points" and "cause the demon to be threatened" and act and reveal itself.[61]

The sacramentals that are recommended by priests and exorcists include things like medals, statues, scapulars, holy water, holy oil, blessed salt, blessed candles, sacred images, and sacred relics.

Medals

Though there are many medals used within the Church, there are two that are highly recommended. The first is the St. Benedict medal, which is particularly efficacious. It is important to get this medal blessed according to the old rite with the full exorcism that is proper to this medal. This medal can be worn with the scapular. Fr. Ripperger recommends having them in the house to add additional protection. The common approach is to bury them in the four corners of your property. Also, if there are problems that are concerning, he recommends placing a medal over every entrance into the house. For some reason, even though they are free to go where they would like, exorcists note that demons are compelled to observe the physical laws to a certain extent, which is why blessings on entranceways are effec-

---

[60] CCC 1667
[61] Fr. Thomas #2

tive. Demons can interfere with technology as well, as exorcists have observed. If your computer, your car, or anything, is acting odd inexplicably, place a St. Benedict medal there.[62]

Fr. Amorth says that it is important to invoke St. Benedict, who is the patron saint of exorcists, and whose great abilities against evil spirits flowed from his sanctity and faith.[63] Fr. Weber points out that most exorcists use the St. Benedict crucifix during the exorcism, and it was recommended to him in his training that he do so as well. The medal has an exorcism prayer inscribed on it, in initials and in Latin.[64] The prayer is:

> The Holy Cross be my light;
> Let not the dragon be my guide.
> Begone Satan!
> Never tempt me with your vanities!
> What you offer me is evil.
> Drink the poison yourself!

When these medals are blessed, they are first exorcised with, among others, the following words, "May all power of the adversary, all assaults and pretensions of Satan, be repulsed and driven afar from these medals." In beseeching the blessing from Our Lord, the priest asks God not only that those who wear this medal "escape by your merciful help all attacks and wiles of the devil," but also that God would "expel all attacks and wiles of the devil from the person who devoutly calls on Your holy name, using these words and signs ascribed to You. May it please You to lead him (her) to the harbor of everlasting salvation."[65]

The second medal that is highly recommended by exorcists, such as Fr. Ripperger, is the Miraculous Medal. This medal, true to the origin of its popular name, is good at bringing about a person's conversion, often in a miraculous fashion. It is also good for conquering evil things in a particular location.[66] Finally, though not a medal, the

---

[62] Ripperger #4
[63] Amorth, 108
[64] Fr. Weber video
[65] *Roman Ritual*, Sanctamissa.org
[66] Ripperger #4

Scapular is a powerful sacramental which is also highly encouraged. Our Lady promises many spiritual benefits to those who wear the scapular in the manner she requires.

Blessed Salt (or "exorcised salt")

Part of the blessing of holy water, in the traditional form, includes the exorcism of salt and the placement of that exorcised salt into the water. This salt may also be used by itself, separate from the holy water. It carries with it a very strong blessing. It is important to have the salt blessed according to the traditional form.[67] This exorcised salt may be sprinkled in a place in the same way that holy water is sprinkled. Fr. Amorth mentions that blessed salt is placed in the corners of rooms where there is suspected diabolical infestation.[68]

Blessed salt may also be used in food, though it should be sprinkled on the food only *after* the food has been cooked.[69] Priests who are chaplains of Catholic schools will often bless all of the salt in the building. Fr. Ripperger shared a story that, when he visited a certain seminary, he blessed all the salt in that place. The next day, two seminarians, about whom they were concerned, decided to leave. He was not certain that there was a direct connection, but it did happen in that order.[70]

In the Roman Ritual, the salt is first exorcised, during which the priest says, "I cast out the demon from you, by the living God, by the true God, by the holy God, by God who ordered you to be thrown into the water-spring by Elisha to heal it of its barrenness." The salt becomes "a medicine for body and soul for all who make use" of it. The salt is also blessed with power against the Evil One. The exorcism says, "May all evil fancies of the foul fiend, his malice and cunning, be driven afar from the place where you are sprinkled." After the exorcism, the salt is blessed with similar words, including, "May

---

[67] The modern blessing of salt is much reduced from its traditional form.
[68] Amorth, 111
[69] Should be placed on the food after cooking in order to avoid tossing any blessed salt into the trash.
[70] Ripperger #7

everything that it touches or sprinkles be freed from uncleanness and any influence of the evil spirit."[71]

Holy Water

Holy water is a well-known and highly used sacramental. It is at the entrance to every Church, is sprinkled on the people during the Sunday Masses of Easter, and is used as the means to impart blessings upon various objects. It is also critical in the rite of exorcism and as a weapon of general spiritual warfare. It is recommended to use holy water blessed in the traditional form, as the blessing in the modern form is greatly reduced when compared to the traditional form. This is important because it is precisely that blessing which is placed on the water which stays with the water and is then imparted to the place in which it is sprinkled.

As Fr. Ripperger describes it, holy water, by means of the new rite of blessing, does have the capacity to drive out the demon, even with a simple blessing, but not to the same extent. The old rite of blessings creates holy water which is much more efficacious, and exorcists have noticed this. Even more efficacious is Epiphany water, which is blessed once a year on Epiphany and, after an elaborate blessing that takes about forty minutes, has a double exorcism blessing on it. Father recommends spreading holy water regularly throughout the house, especially if there are teenagers in the house. Weekly or monthly is a sufficient frequency.[72]

Holy water may be consumed by those having problems like particular temptations, obsessions, or possessions, and can help with illnesses that seem to have no natural cause. It is important that the holy water which is consumed is fresh. In a parish, the holy water that is available for the faithful typically sits out for a long period of time. If you would like to acquire holy water for the purposes of consuming it, it is best to bring fresh bottles of water to the priest for him to bless. Holy water is also useful in cases where the possession is connected to ingesting cursed food. The person may convulse and spit thick saliva during the exorcism if that is the case. Consuming

---

[71] *Roman Ritual*, EWTN.com
[72] Ripperger #4

holy water, blessed salt, and blessed oil will then be helpful for the person.[73]

There are many ways that the faithful may utilize holy water. They can sprinkle it all throughout their homes and on their possessions, particularly on anything new that enters the home. They can sprinkle it in and on their cars to renew the blessing that the priest has, hopefully, already placed on it. Priests also recommend blessing yourself with holy water before bed. If you have had any bad dreams, particularly if they seem to have had a diabolical component, it is advised to sprinkle holy water on your head and senses before going to sleep.[74]

St. Teresa of Avila utilized holy water frequently in her struggles with the devil. In her autobiography, she describes how, after some of her nuns "sprinkled a great deal of holy water," she "saw a huge crowd of [devils] running away as quickly as though they were about to fling themselves down a steep place."[75] She also gives us a remarkable passage about her reliance on this powerful sacramental. She says,

> "From long experience I have learned that there is nothing like holy water to put devils to flight and prevent them from coming back again. They also flee from the Cross, but return; so holy water must have great virtue. For my own part, whenever I take it, my soul feels a particular and most notable consolation. In fact, it is quite usual for me to be conscious of a refreshment which I cannot possibly describe, resembling an inward joy which comforts my whole soul. This is not fancy, or something which has happened to me only once: it has happened again and again and I have observed it most attentively. It is, let us say, as if someone very hot and thirsty were to drink from a jug of cold water: he would feel the refreshment throughout his body. I often reflect on the great importance of everything ordained by the

---

[73] Amorth, 67

[74] In addition to that, there is a very good and helpful prayer called "Commission of the Care of Soul and Body" in Fr. Ripperger's *Deliverance Prayers for Use by the Laity*, that can accompany this additional protection.

[75] *Life of Teresa*, 175

Church and it makes me very happy to find that those words of the Church are so powerful that they impart their power to the water and make it so very different from water which has not been blessed."[76]

As St. Teresa mentions, the blessing on holy water is quite powerful. In the Roman Ritual, the water is first exorcised, then a very small amount of blessed salt is mixed in, and then it is blessed. The exorcism includes a petition that the water be "empowered to drive afar all power of the enemy, in fact, to root out and banish the enemy himself, along with his fallen angels." It continues, asking God that the water will

"serve to cast out demons and to banish disease. May everything that this water sprinkles in the homes and gatherings of the faithful be delivered from all that is unclean and hurtful; let no breath of contagion hover there, no taint of corruption; let all the wiles of the lurking enemy come to nothing."

The final part of the blessing includes the petition for Our Lord to:

"let the light of Your kindness shine upon it, and to hallow it with the dew of Your mercy; so that wherever it is sprinkled and Your holy name is invoked, every assault of the unclean spirit may be baffled, and all dread of the serpent's venom be cast out."

With the knowledge of the blessing which holy water carries with it, it would be advisable that Catholics have a bottle of holy water in every room of their house. Not only would this make it easy to find the holy water should there be some sort of disturbance in the home, but it would also encourage a devotion to this sacramental, and an increase in the virtue of humility, as we constantly realize our dependence on God's blessing and protection.

---

[76] *Life of Teresa*, 173

Blessed Candles

Blessed candles, also referred to as votive candles, are candles that have been blessed in the traditional form which includes a prayer of exorcism. These candles, when burned, drive demons out of the air and out of the house in which the candle resides. Blessed candles function in the same way as blessed incense, whose smoke also drives demons out of the air and the dwelling place. Fr. Ripperger recommends that every candle in your house be blessed.[77] The Roman Ritual blessing on candles includes the following petition:

> "Let the blessing that they receive from the sign of the holy cross be so effectual that, wherever they are lighted or placed, the princes of darkness may depart in trembling from all these places, and flee in fear, along with all their legions, and never more dare to disturb or molest those who serve you."

Demons are permitted to occupy all aspects of the natural world: the air, water, areas underground, dwelling places, the atmosphere, etc. Fr. Ripperger shared a story that demonstrates how demons can also occupy the air in the atmosphere and can stir up violent storms. In Tulsa, Oklahoma, one summer, the area was warned to take cover as two tornadoes touched down nearby. Instead, Father decided to pray an exorcism against storms and tempests. He then checked the news and heard, as he described it, "the newscasters baffled at the fact that the tornadoes just vanished from the air."[78] Fr. Ripperger added that he has heard of this happening to many priests.

A priest friend of mine told me a story related to the path of a hurricane, which changed suddenly after he offered similar prayers. Inspired by what I have personally learned while studying Fr. Ripperger's teachings, and speaking to priest friends well-versed in spiritual warfare matters, I used the binding prayer[79] against a couple of violent and tornado-prone storms that emerged in my area several summers ago. Each time, while watching the storm approach on the

---

[77] Ripperger #4
[78] Ripperger #7
[79] Indirect binding prayer: "Jesus, I ask You to bind…"

radar on my computer, the strong line of storms parted suddenly and went around our small town. While we were, each time, predicted to endure very high winds, downed trees, small hail, and possible tornadoes and power outages, it was reduced to a light rain and a small breeze. It seems that through this binding prayer, in combination with the burial of the blessed palms of Saint Peter Verona,[80] this protection over our property has endured, since this protection has impacted all violent thunderstorm activity ever since.

Sacred Images

Images of Our Lord and Our Lady and the saints powerfully convey the reality of the Person or person signified. As such, as Fr. Ripperger says, sacred images in the home annoy the demons.[81] He recommends that we have them in our homes and wear them on our person, as we are able. Fr. Amorth also recommends keeping sacred images and statues on your person and in your home, as a reminder to ask them for their intercession and protection and to imitate their holiness.[82] St. Louis de Montfort recommends carrying statues in processions, or carrying a small statue of Our Lady, as "an effective protection against the evil one."[83]

Regarding statues, these are recommended in the same manner as any sacred image. In the discussion of statues, it is appropriate to issue the caution, which Fr. Ripperger also does in his talks,[84] about the popular yet superstitious practice of burying the statue of Saint Joseph in order to sell a house. Contrary to the good will of people, this custom is superstitious. This is clear when examining one form of this practice, which involves using the statue in ways that are not proper to its purpose and which are ritualistic. This includes burying the statue upside down, near the "For Sale" sign, facing the road, and utilizing prayers that tell St. Joseph that he will not be freed from the ground

---

[80] Traditionally blessed on his feast day with the intention of granting protection against natural disasters, especially the weather, and diabolical infestation of homes.

[81] Ripperger #4

[82] Amorth, 90

[83] *True Devotion*, 117

[84] Ripperger #4

until the house sells. Instead, we should place the statue in a prominent place in the home and pray to him for his intercession.

A great means of utilizing sacred images is to have the Sacred Heart of Jesus and the Immaculate Heart of Mary enthroned in your home and to consecrate your family to Jesus and Mary. The Roman Ritual contains a rite of enthronement and a blessing of the Sacred Heart of Jesus. During the enthronement, among many other petitions, the priest asks that Our Lord "let no evil spirits approach this place but drive them far away. Let your angels of peace take over and put down all wicked strife." While the enthronement itself does not have an indulgence attached to it, the Consecration to Our Lord does, according the current Manual of Indulgences.

Relics are also helpful and should be placed throughout the house. As it is a Catholic custom to give special attention to saints on their feast days, it is also recommended to venerate, on the proper feast day, the relic of any saint which you may possess in your home. Relics in general should be given regular and due attention. In addition to obtaining the special help of that saint, relics are very powerful against diabolical activity, as seen in exorcisms. They are also, as can be seen in the ministry of "Treasures of the Church," very powerful instruments through which Our Lord chooses to bestow healings and other wonderful blessings.[85]

Holy Oil

Holy oil is also a powerful sacramental with a traditional blessing that includes an exorcism. This exorcised oil is not the oil used for the Sacraments but is a separate sacramental approved by the Church. This oil is extra virgin olive oil and may be used in food and by parents to bless their children.

The Roman Ritual contains both an exorcism and a blessing over the oil. In the exorcism, it says,

"Let the adversary's power, the devil's legions, and all Satan's attacks and machinations be dispelled and driven afar from

---

[85] https://www.treasuresofthechurch.com/healing

this creature, oil. Let it bring health in body and mind to all who use it."

In the blessing, it asks that those who use it

"may be delivered from all suffering, all infirmity, and all wiles of the enemy. Let it be a means of averting any kind of adversity from man, made in your image and redeemed by the precious blood of your Son, so that he may never again suffer the sting of the ancient serpent."

Fr. Ripperger gives several ways that this sacramental may be used. It may be used on the forehead of the child when parents give them a blessing, which he recommends doing regularly. It may also be used in food, in a similar way to blessed salt, after the food is cooked, such as on salads. It would be a sacrilege to pour it out and it should be wiped up after use. It may be placed on anything which is being influenced by the demonic. The father of the family should make the sign of the cross with the oil, silently, on all the entrances to the house.[86] This is similar to, though distinct from, what Fr. Thomas mentions is done in an exorcism. The exorcist seals all the doors of the Church with chrism so the demon cannot leave once expelled from the person.[87]

The Angelic Warfare Confraternity

This is an ancient Confraternity, officially founded in 1727 by Pope Benedict XII. It unofficially began after the death of St. Thomas Aquinas, after whom it takes its inspiration. It is a Confraternity devoted to helping its members achieve chastity according to their state in life. Numerous saints have been members of this Confraternity, including St. Aloysius Gonzaga and Bl. Pier Giorgio Frassati.

In the life of St. Thomas Aquinas, his early devotion to his religious vocation and to purity and chastity were greatly tested or, perhaps more fitting to say, assaulted by his family who opposed his

---

[86] Ripperger #4
[87] See page 145.

decision. In their final desperate attempt to dissuade him from his vocation to the religious life, they imprisoned him and sent a prostitute into his room to seduce him. Immediately, he grabbed a bundle of burning twigs from the fireplace and chased the woman out of his room. After closing the door, he drew a Cross on the door with the smoldering twigs. At that moment, he fell into a vision, where two angels appeared to him and girded him with a cord around his waist and, in so doing, obtained for him the grace of perfect chastity.

This event was known to people in his day and, after his death, the cord was displayed for veneration. People touched cords of their own to this cord and wore them around their waists, in imitation of St. Thomas and seeking his intercession. The Church later instituted this Confraternity and also permitted the use of a medal which was printed to honor this angelic event and grace. The Angelic Warfare Confraternity is now in the keeping of the Dominican Order. Any Dominican priest, or a priest who has received permission from them, may enroll individuals in the Confraternity.

There have been many good fruits and special graces given to those who have enrolled and taken up this devotion. Like the other sacramentals mentioned, the blessing of the cord and medal carry with it great protections from Our Lord. The blessing contains such wording as:

> "By means of the sacred cord of St. Thomas, grant to us who implore Your help through his intercession that we may successfully overcome the temptations of body and soul and come to be crowned with perpetual purity and integrity among the choirs of angels."

Part of the blessing on the cord and medals says,

> "So that whoever reverently carries and wears them around his waist (bears and wears them) may be purified from all uncleanness of mind and body."

After the cord and medal have been presented to the individual, the priest says, among other things,

"May the Lord gird you with the cincture of purity, and by the merits of St. Thomas Aquinas, extinguish within you every evil desire."

For those who are interested in enrolling in the Angelic Warfare Confraternity, speak to your pastor about doing so, or contact the Dominicans for more information.[88] Purity and chastity are virtues that every single Christian in all states of life must establish in order to protect the grace of salvation which Our Lord has bestowed upon us. To drive home this point, the words of St. Alphonsus Liguori are very helpful to reflect upon. He says,

"Whenever the devil tempts us, let us place our entire confidence in the divine assistance, and let us recommend ourselves to Jesus Christ, and to the Most Holy Mary. We ought to do this particularly as often as we are tempted against chastity; for this is the most terrible of all temptations, and is the one by which the devil gains the most victories. We have not the strength to preserve chastity; this strength must come from God."[89]

He adds,

"The occasion of sins of the flesh, in particular, is like a veil placed before the eyes, which prevents the soul from seeing either its resolutions, or the lights received from God, or the truths of eternity: in a word, it makes it forget everything, and almost blinds it."[90]

Binding Prayers

As mentioned in a previous section,[91] Christians have the authority to use what are called binding prayers. These must be used only within the authority structure established by God. It is a self-

---

[88] AngelicWarfareConfraternity.org
[89] *Preparation for Death*, 314
[90] *Preparation for Death*, 319
[91] see page 93 and following.

exorcism, similar to what Our Lord did against St. Peter.[92] The binding prayer can be as simple and direct as this, saying "Get behind me, Satan!" The more complete form of this prayer is, "In the Name of Jesus, I bind you, spirit of _____, and I cast you to the foot of the Cross to be judged by Our Lord."

Fr. Ripperger offers a lot of good advice on the use of binding prayers. In the binding prayer, name the behavior with which you are tempted. It could be sloth, if you are feeling lazy and unmotivated, or sadness, if it is an emotion that burdens you. The binding prayer can be used on certain other people than simply yourself. Within a marriage, there is an authority structure and also an exchange of bodily rights with the spouse. If one of the spouses is in need, the other can say binding prayers against that with which the spouse is struggling. Parents can also say these prayers over their children. To a certain extent, you can use these direct binding prayers over other people outside of your family, but there is a risk of retaliation.[93] It is best to start using these prayers within your family first and, when spiritually strong, discern if and when to use them over others.[94]

When binding and removing the demon with this prayer, it is important to send them to the Cross for judgment, so they receive their sentence from God instead of continuing to roam around the earth.[95] St. Alphonsus comments on this passage, adding a helpful emphasis on the malice of the demon. He says, "When banished from a soul, the devil finds no repose, and does everything in his power to return: he even calls companions to his aid; and if he succeeds in re-entering, the second fall of that soul will be far more ruinous than the first."[96]

Ultimately, it is unknown where the demon goes after the liberation. Fr. Amorth says he sends the demon, in the name of Jesus, "to return to the eternal inferno or to go under the Cross of Jesus," but it is only Our Lord who gives the final command and destination.[97] Fr. Thomas has a very fascinating insight as to the behavior of the de-

---

[92] Matthew 16:23

[93] A priest-friend who helps with exorcisms told me that they always say prayers against retaliation after they conclude an exorcism.

[94] Ripperger #4

[95] Cf. Luke 11:24f

[96] *Preparation for Death*, 313

[97] Amorth, 106

mons at this point, and what he does to ensure the demon does not have a chance to roam around, prowling on more souls. He says,

> "The exorcisms happen only in the Church. The Blessed Sacrament is exposed on the altar along with relics of the saints. They seal every door with chrism so that the demons are not permitted to leave. When they're delivered, they're assigned to the foot of the Cross to be bound there. Otherwise they could just go off and find someone else to attach themselves too."[98]

Fasting

Our Lord teaches that some demons cannot be cast out except by prayer and fasting.[99] As St. Francis de Sales says, "Besides the ordinary effect of fasting in raising the mind, subduing the flesh, confirming goodness, and obtaining a heavenly reward, it is also a great matter to be able to control greediness, and to keep the sensual appetites and the whole body subject to the law of the Spirit." He recommends that, if we are able to fast, we do so beyond what the Church requires. Still, he says that, even if we are "able to do but little, the enemy nevertheless stands more in awe of those whom he knows can fast."[100] Fr. Amorth adds that, "Beyond a certain limit, the devil is not able to resist the power of prayer and fasting."[101]

St. Alphonsus warns against abandoning a spirit of fasting. He states, "As fasting prepares the mind for the contemplation of God and of eternal good, so intemperance diverts it from holy thoughts." He adds that St. John Chrysostom taught that "the glutton, like an overloaded ship, moves with difficulty; and that, in the first tempest of temptation, he is in danger of being lost."[102] A lack of temperance and control of the appetite leads to an inclination to indulge the other senses as well. This exposes the soul to many moral dangers, the worst of which is an assault on chastity. Sins of the flesh, as St. Al-

---

[98] Fr. Thomas #2
[99] Mark 9:29
[100] *Devout Life*, 134
[101] Amorth, 24
[102] *True Spouse of Christ*, 140

phonsus says, are so powerful that they cause the soul to nearly forget everything related to God and become almost blind.[103] However, as the saints experience, the devil does not tempt us toward lust once he is thwarted by temperance.[104]

Know Thyself

This section will cover different aspects related to self-awareness, and not necessarily in the introspective sense. We should know, for example, a good deal about our family history and about where we currently live.

Exorcists recommend that you inquire about the previous renters or owners of your home or apartment. Fr. Ripperger adds that we should inquire about our neighborhood as well. When grave sins or occultic practices occur, demons can become involved. As Father adds, "Demons love places, and they get attached as a result of sin and evil."[105] Fr. Thomas says that he asks people about the previous owners of the home because he has seen many cases where the prior owners were involved in Satanism and the occult. Often, they will leave signs in the home which will remain after they have left.[106]

To explain this point, Fr. Thomas tells a story about a time when Fr. Grob was called in to help with a situation in an apartment building. Everyone was getting sick on a particular floor and the apartment owners could not figure out why, even after calling in various engineers to inspect the place. After finding a pentagram carved on the wall in an office on that floor, they called Fr. Grob. He exorcised the whole place and, after that, there were no more problems.[107] These are examples explaining why the Church advises that, right after moving into a new home or apartment, we should have the priest over to bless it. If you become aware that any occult or Satanic practices have happened in the house, then call the priest to do a further exorcism.[108]

---

[103] *Preparation for Death,* 319
[104] *True Spouse of Christ,* 141
[105] Ripperger #4
[106] Fr. Thomas #2
[107] Fr. Thomas #2
[108] Ripperger #4

Our family history is also important to know about as it could be a source for diabolical disturbances. If deceased relatives were in the occult or Satanism, the demon may have entered the family line as a generational spirit. If a family member was involved in Freemasonry, exorcists take that very seriously. Anyone involved in Freemasonry is in a state of mortal sin and, as would be obvious, Catholics are forbidden to be Freemasons. A lie has been spread in the last many decades that the Church has changed this teaching: she has not. The Church has condemned Freemasonry as far back as the eighteenth century and as recently as 1983,[109] where she repeated that Catholics are forbidden to be associated with Freemasonry.

One of the countless grave concerns comes from the fact that, as part of the higher levels of membership in the Freemasons, a member will invoke a generational curse on his family line, from himself going forward. Fr. Ripperger says, "Even if you have a family member in the low levels of the Freemasons, you should still do the prayers to break the Freemasonic curse. All they have to do is enter into the lowest level and the family can become subject to the curse."[110] This does not mean that you have it, but you will want to say the prayers to break the Freemasonic curse nonetheless.[111] Fr. Thomas says that, when he finds out there is Freemasonry in the family of a person, he has that person pray the entire prayer to break the Freemasonic curse, just as a precaution.[112]

The Power of Our Lady

St. Alphonsus Liguori, one of the great Doctors of the Church, eloquently states the power and authority that Our Lady possesses as a result of her intimacy with Our Lord, her Son. Her victory over the devil is a source of hope for us, for she is our Mother, to whom Our Lord entrusted every one of His disciples.[113] Faithfully embracing her as our Mother, we can then personally experience the fruits of her triumph over evil.

---

[109] *Declaration on Masonic Associations*, Congregation for the Doctrine of the Faith
[110] Ripperger #6
[111] visit http://www.sensustraditionis.org/Freemasonic.pdf
[112] Fr. Thomas #3
[113] John 19:27

St. Alphonsus says,

> "Mary, then, was this great and valiant woman, who con-
> quered the devil and crushed his head by bringing down his
> pride, as it was foretold by God Himself: 'she shall crush his
> head.' Saint Bernard remarks, this proud spirit, in spite of
> himself, was beaten down and trampled under foot by this
> most Blessed Virgin; so that, as a slave conquered in war, he
> is forced always to obey the commands of this Queen. 'Beat-
> en down and trampled under the feet of Mary, he endures a
> wretched slavery'."[114]

Through her virtues, Mary obtained a victory over all the evil
spirits. As such, St. Alphonsus labels her not only Queen of Heaven
but also Queen of hell, a title also used by St. Bernadine of Sienna,
among others.[115] One Queenship by exaltation, another by conquest.
St. Alphonsus adds that Mary "tames and crushes" the devils, and
"snatches" souls from their grasp, presenting them to Her Son.[116]

A true devotion to Our Lady will secure us in this spiritual warfare because, if we love her, the demons will fear us all the more. All
the demons fell in opposition to one aspect of the plan that God revealed to them at the first moment of their creation. Satan fell
because of Our Lady, out of opposition to her role in the plan of the
salvation of the human race. All the demons fell in union with Satan
so, regardless of what their individual sins were, they hate her because
her role and holiness is at the root of their rebellion. As Fr. Thomas
remarks, this hatred of the Blessed Mother is so intense that her prayers are often more powerful than the rite of exorcism itself.[117]

St. Louis de Montfort says that demons have been forced, in exorcisms, contrary to their preference, to admit that "they fear one of
her pleadings for a soul more than the prayers of all the saints, and
one of her threats more than all their other torments."[118] A prayer to
Our Lady, under the title Our Lady of Perpetual Succour, conveys the

---

[114] *Glories of Mary*, 117
[115] Ibid. 116
[116] Ibid. 119
[117] Fr. Thomas #2
[118] *True Devotion*, 52

sentiments of hope which the power of Our Lady communicates to souls. Within that prayer are the words, "For, if thou protect me, I fear nothing; not from my sins, because thou wilt obtain for me the pardon of them; nor from the devils, because thou art more powerful than all hell together."[119]

Fr. Ripperger says that Our Lady has perfect coercive power over the demons. As a result, when she is sent to assist in an exorcism, the possession is simply over.[120] Some saints are sent for similar reasons, to help with exorcisms, but Our Lady is on a level that no saint has reached or could ever try to reach.[121] Fr. Ripperger particularly recommends invoking Our Lady under the title "Our Lady of Sorrows." This title relates to the sufferings that the Blessed Mother endured as the Mother of the Redeemer, notably beginning at the Presentation of Our Lord in the Temple. At that moment, Simeon prophesied to her, saying:

And thy own soul a sword shall pierce, that, out of many hearts, thoughts may be revealed.[122]

As Fr. Ripperger states, the Fathers of the Church teach that, at this moment, Simeon recounted to Mary all of the sufferings that Christ would endure. This privileged intimacy also merited for her insights into God's plan, including things that are going on in our lives, such as with generational spirits. Father compares this to how we tell others, whom we trust and love in a special way, things that we would not tell anyone else. If we are struggling with an obsession, oppression, or generational spirit, he recommends that we pray every day to Our Lady of Sorrows. It will not take long for her to make the matter clearer to you.[123]

St. Bridget of Sweden has handed on to the Church the devotion to Our Lady of Sorrows. In it, Our Lady made many promises to the faithful who meditate on the Seven Sorrows of Mary. She said, among others, "I will give them as much as they ask for, as long as it

---

[119] Raccolta
[120] See page 66.
[121] Ripperger #7
[122] Luke 2:35 DR
[123] Ripperger #9

does not oppose the adorable will of my divine Son or the sanctification of their souls," and "I will defend them in their spiritual battles with the infernal enemy and I will protect them at every instant of their lives." According to St. Alphonsus, further revelations about the spiritual benefits of this devotion were given by Our Lord to St. Elizabeth. Of the four principal graces which Our Lord mentioned, notable here is the promise "that He would commit such devout clients to the hands of Mary, with the power to dispose of them in whatever manner she might please, and to obtain for them all the graces she might desire."[124]

St. Louis de Montfort says that, "Only Mary knows how to fill our minds with the thought of God."[125] St. Bernard adds, "When Mary supports you, you will not fail. With her as your protector, you will have nothing to fear. With her as your guide, you will not grow weary. When you win her favour, you will reach the port of heaven."[126] According to St. Bonaventure, for those devoted to her, "She prevents their virtues from fading away, their merits from being wasted and their graces from being lost. She prevents the devils from doing them harm."[127]

Patron Saints

The assistance of the saints is a vital aid in the journey to salvation. Patron saints are first those after whom you have been named and those for whom you have a particular devotion. Fr. Ripperger says, interestingly, that God will often give the grace to a person, who is struggling with an obsession or is possessed, to have a devotion to the very saint who is the nemesis of the demon who is attacking them. As a result, the person is already equipped for the battle.[128] He says that patron saints also include the saint after whom the parish is named where you attend, the saint whose name is taken at Confirmation, the patron saint of the Diocese and country where you live, as

---

[124] *Glories of Mary*, 417
[125] *True Devotion*, 165
[126] Ibid. 174
[127] Ibid.
[128] Ripperger #7

well as the patron saints of the members of your family.[129] It is help-ful to have a devotion to all of these saints.

Guardian Angels

"The servant of Eliseus was struck with terror when he saw the city encompassed with enemies; but the saint inspired him with courage, saying, 'Fear not; for there are more with us than with them.' He then showed him an army of angels sent by God to defend the city."[130]

Our Guardian Angels are assigned to us by God Himself. St. Thomas Aquinas says that "the guardianship of the angels is an effect of Divine providence in regard to man."[131] As a result, protecting us is the mission they have fully accepted and carry out in complete obedience to Almighty God, animated with sanctifying grace and the theological virtues. They are powerful protectors who behold God face to face, endowed with intellects naturally incomprehensibly more powerful than our own, which are also infused with knowledge from God. Not only are they able to communicate with us, but they constantly intercede for us with God.

St. Thomas also adds that "the angel guardian never forsakes a man entirely, but sometimes he leaves him in some particular, for instance by not preventing him from being subject to some trouble, or even from falling into sin, according to the ordering of Divine judgments."[132] Fr. Ripperger says that, in the beginning, our Guardian Angels were only given a certain amount of authority over us. By praying to them, we increase that authority, permitting them to act more powerfully in our lives.[133] Similar to Our Lady of Sorrows, our Guardian Angels know the spiritual battle that is happening all around us, and in particular which demons are attacking us. They can provide essential aid in warding off these diabolical influences. As Fr. Amorth says, invoke your Guardian Angel often, "who protect us

---

[129] Ripperger #4

[130] *Preparation for Death*, 98. Eliseus is the prophet Elisha. In-text quotation is from 2 Kings 6:16.

[131] Summa 1, Q. 113, A 6

[132] Summa 1, Q. 113, A 6

[133] Ripperger #4

from dangers and who give us the proper suggestions at the right moments."[134]

Fr. Ripperger says that, in addition to our own Guardian Angel, we should also have a devotion to the Guardian Angel of our family members, in particular the Guardian Angel of our spouse. We receive a Guardian Angel at our conception[135] but, as Father says, are then given an additional Guardian Angel to protect our marriage or priestly vocation, depending on which path we choose. God also assigns a Guardian Angel over the parish, the town, the local region, and corporations.[136]

Auxilium Christianorum

The spiritual association called *Auxilium Christianorum* is designed to provide support for both priests and laity in the work of spiritual deliverance. For priests, it provides the aid of the prayers of the other members of the association so that their priestly work in driving out the demonic is effective and they remain protected. For the laity who join, it provides the aid of the prayers of the association in order to protect them from diabolical influence.

The priests who began the association did so after becoming acutely aware of the difficulties that good people were having at protecting themselves and their families from the influences of evil, both from the world and from the demonic realm. They realized that both the laity and the priests who work in the ministry of exorcism and deliverance needed extra support. Fr. Ripperger speaks highly of this group and notes that they have seen tremendous benefits for people who join.

It is recommended to get the approval of your pastor or spiritual director before joining due to the fact that "members often experience an increase in their spiritual lives" after joining. This is not a negative thing, because, as they say on their website, the association is there to protect the members, who "often experience a decrease in demonic

---

[134] Amorth, 19

[135] St. Thomas held "with some degree of probability" that the child was protected in the womb by the mother's Guardian Angel. The debate then was over whether the child received an Angel at birth or at Baptism. Now it is commonly held to be given at conception.

[136] Ripperger #7

influence in their own personal lives over the course of time."[137] There are requirements for recitation of certain daily prayers and an increase in certain devotions. The requirements are not burdensome, and the benefits are very helpful in this age which some exorcists plainly call "satanic."[138]

Simply search for *Auxilium Christianorum* online, and you will find out more information.

This spiritual association fulfills, in spirit if not in practice, the advice of the *Ritual of Exorcism,* as Fr. Amorth discusses it. He encourages all of the faithful to help those who have experienced diabolical influence and have been liberated. He also highlights where the *Ritual* says, "It is advised that the faithful, once liberated, either alone or with family members, give thanks to God for the peace they have obtained. May it stay with them as long as they persevere in prayer, read the Sacred Scripture, receive the sacraments of Penance and the Eucharist, and practice a Christian life rich in charity, good works and fraternal love."[139] It would seem, then, that this spiritual association is ideal for such individuals.

The prophetic nature of the teachings of St. Louis de Montfort also seems to connect to our times and to this association. For those unfamiliar, the prayers of the *Auxilium Christianorum* are intensely Marian and spiritual warfare focused. With its additional emphasis on both St. Michael the Archangel and Our Lady under the title *Virgo Potens* (Virgin Most Powerful), the following passage from the writings of St. Louis de Montfort seems ever so fitting to incorporate here. In his classic work, *True Devotion to Mary*, he states,

> "But Mary's power over the evil spirits will especially shine forth in the latter times, when Satan will lie in wait for her heel, that is, for her humble servants and her poor children whom she will rouse to fight against him. In the eyes of the world they will be little and poor and, like the heel, lowly in the eyes of all, down-trodden and crushed as is the heel by the other parts of the body. But in compensation for this they

---

[137] http://auxiliumchristianorum.org/faq/
[138] Carlin, 3
[139] Amorth, 83

will be rich in God's graces, which will be abundantly bestowed on them by Mary. They will be great and exalted before God in holiness. They will be superior to all creatures by their great zeal and so strongly will they be supported by divine assistance that, in union with Mary, they will crush the head of Satan with their heel, that is, their humility, and bring victory to Jesus Christ."[140]

To conclude this Chapter on protecting your spiritual life, let us recall the admonition of St. Raphael the Archangel, from the Book of Tobit, where he describes the goodness of giving thanks to God, of doing good, of fasting and giving alms, of performing works of charity, of the reward for prayer and corporal works of mercy:

Then the angel called the two of them privately and said to them: "Praise God and give thanks to him; exalt him and give thanks to him in the presence of all the living for what he has done for you. It is good to praise God and to exalt his name, worthily declaring the works of God. Do not be slow to give him thanks. It is good to guard the secret of a king, but gloriously to reveal the works of God. Do good, and evil will not overtake you. Prayer is good when accompanied by fasting, almsgiving, and righteousness. A little with righteousness is better than much with wrongdoing. It is better to give alms than to treasure up gold. For almsgiving delivers from death, and it will purge away every sin. Those who perform deeds of charity and of righteousness will have fulness of life; but those who commit sin are the enemies of their own lives... And so, when you and your daughter-in-law Sarah prayed, I brought a reminder of your prayer before the Holy One; and when you buried the dead, I was likewise present with you. When you did not hesitate to rise and leave your dinner in order to go and lay out the dead, your good deed was not hidden from me, but I was with you. So now God sent me..."[141]

---

[140] *True Devotion*, 54
[141] Tobit 12:6-10,12-14

Compendium X

+ Christians are born for combat and, with the graces that Our Lord bestows on us through His Church, we have all the arms we need to do battle.
+ Allowing Our Lord to heal us, and remaining obedient to Him at all times, will obtain for us the strength we require.
+ The more devout and holy we are, the more the devil fears us and is powerless against us.
+ The principal means of protection is to remain in a state of grace with a deep faith, which is nurtured and supported by frequent reception of Holy Communion and Confession.
+ A daily spiritual focus should include an emphasis on the virtue of humility and the need for prayer and meditation.
+ Catholics should nurture a devout and frequent use of the sacramentals of the Church, such as approved medals, statues, scapulars, holy water, holy oil, blessed salt, blessed candles, sacred images, and sacred relics.
+ Fasting will increase how repugnant we are to the demons and help to drive them away, with the help of a prudent and frequent use of binding prayers.
+ It is important to know the history of your family, your neighborhood, your home, and areas you frequent to ensure that no diabolical doorways have been opened by means of these.
+ A devotion to Our Lady is one of the most powerful means to obtain an abundance of grace from Our Lord and protection against the workings of the Evil One.
+ In addition to Our Lady and the saints, Catholics should nurture a devotion to and a friendship with their Guardian Angels, who are much more powerful than most people realize.

Chapter Eleven

Consorting with Evil

There are many people in the world today who willingly open themselves up to the devil. Some do so in a mocking manner and do not take the devil seriously, while others are truly open to or desire to receive an answer from the diabolical realm. Juvenile curiosities are often infused with a diabolical element. Countless celebrities have openly embraced the assistance of Satan and spirits in their work of attaining and securing fame. Satanist groups now openly profess their beliefs and perform public ritualistic displays of their hatred of the Catholic Faith.

Exorcists are seeing a rise in diabolical oppression and obsession related to sin, witchcraft, Satanism, and the occult. As mentioned before, exorcists tend to think this is also due to a tremendous increase in the use of pornography and other grave things of that sort. Pornography use is, as Fr. Ripperger puts it, "off the charts." He relates that exorcists have learned that Satanists have taught pornographers that if they would curse the master copy of the pornographic video, whoever watches a copy may become subject to the same curse. Father told the story of a man who had become possessed through the use of pornography. The demon possessing the man confirmed this detail.[1] The man's possession followed an obsession with finding every film with this specific woman in it.

Pornography can create a very strong diabolical obsession and can be a gateway to possession.[2] Fr. Thomas agrees that pornography "can open doorways to the demonic."[3] The issue of pornography and its potential connection to possession is an issue of universal Church

---

[1] Ripperger #2
[2] Ripperger #2
[3] https://www.catholic.com/magazine/print-edition/interview-with-an-exorcist

concern. In 2018, for example, an annual exorcism course at the Pontifical Regina Apostolorum University discussed to what extent demonic influence exists in the use of pornography.[4]

Rise in the Occult

As exorcists across the world attest, curiosity about and recourse to the occult is greatly on the rise. Fr. Thomas states that twenty-five percent of people in Italy in 2005 were involved in the occult. He said those same trends were appearing in the US as well.[5] This Italian statistic stayed the same in 2018, and is still experiencing a "surge in occult activity," such as recourse to tarot card readers, fortune tellers, and astrologers.[6]

The spokesman for the International Association of Exorcists, Dr. Cascioli, in 2012, described the increase in diabolical activity as a "pastoral emergency," adding that the "number of disturbances of extraordinary demonic activity is on the rise."[7] He repeated this same concern in 2016.[8] Different forms of paganism, witchcraft, idolatry, and the occult are all gateway sins to all levels of diabolical influence, including possession. Fr. Fortea, speaking about the different entry points for demons, says, "As you see, we have many possibilities. It is a very mysterious world. When we exorcists are interviewed, we have a very simple answer: avoid the occult, and that is true."[9]

According to a 2008 and 2018 religion survey,[10] the number of witches is significantly rising in the United States. In 1990, there were 8,400 Wiccans, which grew to 340,000 in 2008. It is now, in 2018, between 1 and 1.5 million. This number does not include all

---

[4] https://www.catholicnewsagency.com/news/exorcism-course-to-study-link-between-porn-and-demonic-influence-30162

[5] Fr. Thomas #2

[6] https://catholicherald.co.uk/news/2018/03/06/demonic-activity-is-on-the-rise-in-italy-says-exorcist/

[7] https://www.catholicnewsagency.com/news/exorcisms-on-the-rise-occult-activity-sparks-pastoral-emergency-18264

[8] https://www.telegraph.co.uk/news/2016/09/26/urgent-need-for-more-exorcists-as-increasing-number-of-people-da/

[9] http://www.ncregister.com/daily-news/halloween-the-catholic-faith-and-the-occult

[10] Study by Quartz, collecting data from Connecticut's Trinity College and Pew Research Center, in 2018. https://www.lifesitenews.com/news/report-witchcraft-rising-in-us-as-christianity-declines

forms of witchcraft, as not all witches identify as Wiccan, though this is a significant subset of witches. To demonstrate the significance of this number of Wiccans, there were 1.4 million Presbyterians in 2017. The number of Satanists in the United States is unknown, partly due to the secrecy with which they operate.

When a person first comes to an exorcist, after determining there is a true spiritual issue, the exorcist begins to inquire into the person's life, looking for possible doorways for demons. Many of the people who are diabolically disturbed have opened themselves up through the occult, or through a connection with Satanic cults, or through dabbling in something in the category of the New Age.[11] This curiosity is extremely dangerous. As Fr. Amorth says, curiosity leads the youth into the "myriad tentacles of occultism" and eventually to the door of the exorcist.[12] When young people become interested in Ouija boards or spells, those spirits may actually come to you and hang around. While it is rare for possession to happen immediately, Fr. Fortea says that the person will likely experience "a presence in that moment with the people around the table, and sometimes that presence is around a person of the group for a week or two weeks, but nothing more. Fortunately, because God protects, to be possessed is not so easy."[13]

The rise of the occult also includes a popular acceptance of witchcraft, spells, and the demonic in society. Popular media, such as music and television and literature, are all opening up to more positive portrayals of these occult categories. This is happening all over the world. Fr. Amorth cautions against participating in these things and, in particular, advises the young to avoid horror films. These films "tend to normalize brutal situations, particularly, where the demon is the protagonist" and "can seriously upset fragile minds and stir others to sadistic emulation." Though viewing these films does not directly cause spiritual ills, they can indirectly do so by enticing the person who watches them toward the occult.[14]

In his book, *An Exorcist Tells His Story*, Fr. Amorth, commenting on the presence of witchcraft, spiritism, and the occult on TV, in music, in books, and in newspapers, says, "When I was invited to speak

---

[11] Fr. Thomas #2
[12] Amorth, 81
[13] http://www.ncregister.com/daily-news/halloween-the-catholic-faith-and-the-occult
[14] Amorth, 56

at a few high schools, I was able personally to verify how great is the influence of these tools of Satan on the young. It is unbelievable how widespread are witchcraft and spiritism, in all their forms, in middle and high school. This evil is everywhere, even in small towns."[15]

Though possession is not common in the first instance of dabbling in the occult, serious diabolical influences are more common when the person is also suffering from an emotional or mental instability. Exorcists consistently mention, for example, that victims of abuse are more susceptible to diabolical influence if they approach the occult. Fr. Fortea says, starkly, "A demon is never invoked in vain." He says that, if the person has an open wound, the demon will latch on. Even if the person is not especially vulnerable to the demonic, the invocation of a demon, through a spell or a curse, will always cause harm, both to the one performing and requesting the spell and, only if God permits it, to the one who is the target of the spell.[16]

Satanism Comfortable in Public

The willingness of the world to embrace the demonic is in part aided by the world of fame and drugs. These two powerful escapes from reality are accompanied by testimonies about people's related involvement with the diabolical. Fr. John Corapi, the once-famous priest who had an amazing conversion story, revealed many evil things that he witnessed during his early life chasing fame and drugs. He witnessed witches cursing shipments of drugs coming in on cargo ships from South America and rock bands dedicating their albums to Satan in the recording studio. Bob Dylan suspiciously stated in an interview that he was still performing late in life because he is keeping up his end of the bargain he made "with the Chief Commander...on this earth and in the world we can't see."[17] Beyoncé readily admits in interviews that a spirit animates her when she performs, enabling her to do things that her natural personality does not enable her to do.[18] These are just a few of the many public stories

---

[15] Amorth, *Exorcist Tells*, 53-54

[16] Fortea, 111

[17] Viewable on YouTube through a simple search.

[18] In a BET interview, she speaks about "Sasha," an "alter ego" that enables her to perform in ways she cannot do alone; referred to it as "com[ing] into me" before a performance.

of celebrities willingly involving themselves in spiritism, witchcraft, and Satanism.

Satanists have also begun openly intruding upon the public space which we all enjoy, demanding to lead prayer at city council meetings, setting up monuments on public property, and holding sacrilegious rituals on city streets. The Pensacola City Council, in 2016, permitted the Satanic Temple of West Florida to lead the prayer invocation at the beginning of their meeting. In the same year, in Arizona, the Satanic Temple in Tucson had been permitted to lead the invocation prayer at the upcoming Phoenix City Council meeting. The City Council then voted, first, to stop the practice of the opening prayer and replace it with a moment of silence, voting again later to permit the prayer, but this time only by a chaplain from the city's police and fire departments.

Though still few in number, Steve Hill, an avowed atheist and Satanic temple organizer, ran for a seat in the California state senate in 2016. He received twelve percent of the vote among four Republican and Democratic candidates in his district.

Satanic groups have sought to receive official recognition of their presence both through the above-mentioned right to lead prayer at city council meetings, and through the right to place their monuments on public property alongside other religious monuments.

In the summer of 2015, the Satanic Temple in Oklahoma was almost successful at getting a proposed Baphomet statue permitted to be placed outside the state Capitol, alongside the Ten Commandments monument, which had been in place since 2012. The Ten Commandments monument was then destroyed but was later rebuilt. The Oklahoma Supreme Court then ruled that the new Ten Commandments monument must be removed, which led the Satanic Temple to drop their request and to turn their focus to Arkansas, which had a similar Ten Commandments monument at the state Capitol. In the summer of 2018, the Satanic Temple unveiled an 8-foot-tall bronze statue of Baphomet on the back of a truck at the Arkansas Capital building in front of a cheering crowd. As of this writing, they have not been permitted to place this statue on the grounds of the Capital building.

That same statue had been privately unveiled among Satanists in a warehouse in Detroit in 2015. As was reported by Church Militant, who filmed on location, this event was accompanied by explicit acts of debauchery, perversion, and homosexuality. In order to spare the reader anymore visuals related to this event, please read the article and watch the video at Church Militant for more details, if interested.[19]

In 2018, the Satanic Temple in Chicago was permitted to place a monument, called the "Snaketivity," in the Illinois Capitol rotunda, right next to a Nativity scene, a Christmas tree, and a menorah. The Satanic monument is a black box, with the Satanic logo, an arm holding an apple reaching out above it, and a snake wrapping itself around the arm. A red glow at the base of the arm casts a light onto the figure.

In December 2015, Satanists were given a legal permit to hold a Satanic ritual of desecration against a statue of Our Lady on Christmas Eve in front of Saint Joseph Old Cathedral in Oklahoma City. This event was preceded by a protest of reparation by faithful Catholics from the area. Despite the calls to revoke the permit, the Satanists were permitted to, and did, carry out the sacrilegious event. In addition, Satanic "black masses" have been popping up in California, Oklahoma, and even at Harvard. Some of these events have been thwarted, others have not. One of the events in Oklahoma, in 2014, first involved a lawsuit by the Archdiocese of Oklahoma City seeking to secure the return of a stolen consecrated Host, which the Satanists had intended to desecrate in the ceremony. The lawsuit was successful, and the Host was returned, but the "black mass" still took place.

A final note for this section is the rise of after-school programs that encourage Satanism. The group by the name "After School Satan" has been successful in establishing itself at elementary schools beginning in 2016. The group claims to have established their after-school clubs at elementary schools in Atlanta, Los Angeles, Pensacola, Portland, Salt Lake City, Seattle, Springfield, Tucson, and Washington, D.C. They claim to be dedicated to scientific rationalism and only view Satan as a metaphor of the Eternal Rebel. They intentionally commit blasphemy as, so they say, a way of expressing their refusal to conform to traditional norms of behavior.

---

[19] https://www.churchmilitant.com/news/article/exclusive-reportthe-devil-in-detroit

It might be easy for some to overlook this use of blasphemy as simply a form of shock meant to get attention. However, as St. Alphonsus tells us, blasphemy directly ties us to the work of demons. His words are important to ponder. St. Alphonsus states that "blasphemy proceeds from a bad will, and from a certain hatred conceived against God. Hence the blasphemer renders himself like the damned."[20] The use of blasphemy by Satanists thus makes sense, in that they revel in lifting up Satan as a model to follow. Reflecting on the fact that Christians receive, in the traditional rite of Baptism, blessed salt on their tongue, St. Alphonsus says, first quoting a writer, "'the tongues of Christians [are thus] made, as it were, sacred, and may be accustomed to bless God.' And the blasphemer afterwards makes this tongue, as St. Bernadine says, a sword to pierce the heart of God. Hence the Saint adds that no sin contains in itself so much malice as the sin of blasphemy." Blasphemy is so wretched that St. Alphonsus calls it the "language of Hell." "Thus we may say," he continues, "to every blasphemer: You are from Hell; you are a true disciple of Lucifer; for you speak the language of the damned."[21]

Sinful Curiosity

As New Age practices are on the rise, so is a desire for spiritual autonomy, so to speak, which makes people think that their own ideas and interests about the spiritual realm are valid and beneficial. This can lead to a naïve and dangerous curiosity about things, which opens people up to a vague spiritual realm, outside of the protection of the Church.

One popular practice has been to seek to acquire a "spirit guide" for oneself. These spirit guides are not defined as having any specific attributes and can sometimes present themselves as people who once lived on the earth but are now dead. The idea is appealing to people and many seek them out. This is often tied to recourse to mediums and fortune tellers, who themselves often rely on some sort of spirit guide.

---

[20] *Sermons*, 404
[21] *Sermons*, 403

As Fr. Ripperger describes, when people open themselves up to a spirit guide, only demons will respond, not Angels or saints or the souls of the faithful departed. When this begins, everything will seem fine at first, until the person has had enough of the conversation and says "no" to the demon. At that point, the attitude of the spirit changes completely.[22] The demon had obtained permission to be there after the person let them in, and they want to stay.

Sinful curiosity extends to visiting haunted houses and watching shows and movies about the paranormal. People want to see the ghosts that are reported to dwell in places, but this is a big door-opener to the diabolical. It is a curiosity not simply to see these things but to also desire to know about things that are not necessary for us to know. This is a dangerous curiosity.

Popular practices like the "Charlie, Charlie" game must be completely avoided and parents need to teach their children not to engage in such "games." This, just like the Ouija board, is a form of diabolic channeling and people do become possessed from these practices. We must also stay away from people and locations where these things are occurring. Demons are not contagious, but if we go into a place where they have been given the right to dwell, they could begin to take interest in us. "However," as Fr. Ripperger says, "if you are in a state of mortal sin or have a spiritual life that is not in order, and you go into an infested house, you can get possessed."[23]

Seeking Extraordinary Spiritual Gifts

Similar to sinful curiosity is the desire to receive extraordinary spiritual gifts, such as the ability to heal, speak in tongues, and have visions. The extraordinary gifts that God gives are gratuitous and cannot be merited; they are sheer gifts. It is important that we humbly accept the gifts God gives us while also not seeking them in a prideful way. Fr. Ripperger says that the worst case of possession he has ever dealt with involved a woman who prayed for the gift of tongues and, with an unexpected result, received it: possession. This woman became possessed because she approached the gift of tongues from a

---

[22] Ripperger #1
[23] Ripperger #7

superstitious mindset and her 'prayer' was actually a form of 'channeling.' This is where you 'open up' and 'let the spirits speak through you.' It is a dangerous and prideful form of desiring spiritual power.[24]

Fr. Ripperger also cautions about some practices in the Charismatic renewal movement. While some people in this movement are very serious, certain practices are very problematic. The concept of being 'slain in the spirit,'[25] he says, is not an authentic charismatic gift. The practice of having laymen lay hands on a person, in the manner of a priest, is a superstitious practice and can lead to diabolical obsession and oppression. Fr. Ripperger adds, "Lay people praying with you for deliverance is okay, so long as they are not doing things that are proper to a priest."[26]

Paganism of Eastern Influence

Among the many modern forms of spiritualism are those which have their origin in the East. Among these, two more popular practices are Reiki and Yoga, both of which receive a wide condemnation from exorcists.

Reiki is a popular occultic practice that traces back to a Buddhist technique of channeling good energy. Despite the "good" part, as Fr. Ripperger notes, Reiki is tied to a cult of Osiris, a brutal demon and one of the cruelest. His sin came from the refusal to accept the mercy that Christ wanted to give to men. Practicing Reiki can lead to possession, he adds.[27] In 2018, Bishop Alphonsus Cullinan of the Dioceses of Waterford and Lismore, Ireland, warned of the dangers of Reiki and, at the same time, announced he was taking new initiatives regarding deliverance ministry in his Diocese. In the report, he says that the brother of a Reiki master told him of an account where the Reiki master, working with a person, had a vision of Satan. The Reiki master was "scared out of his wits, dropped the Reiki and went back

---

[24] Ripperger #6

[25] Where a person, after receiving a blessing from a priest, or perhaps a spiritual experience otherwise, falls to the ground as if unconscious, purportedly due to an outpouring of grace.

[26] Ripperger #6, #3

[27] Ripperger #2

to the Church."[28] The USCCB has issued a condemnation of Reiki, saying that those who practice it are "operating in the realm of superstition."[29] As a grave sin against the First Commandment, it is a doorway for the diabolic.

Yoga, despite its intense popularity all throughout the country, is also from the occult.[30] Experts in the field of Yoga, both inside and outside of Hinduism, as well as Hindu practitioners, say the physical movements of Yoga are invocations of, and worship of, Eastern deities, like the Sun god. Further, these experts say that the physical dimension of Yoga cannot be separated from the spiritual dimension. Certain Yoga exercises, such as the "Sun Salutations," are clearly religious in their sequence, rhythm, and intent. As a result, it would be a sin, objectively speaking, to do that which is offensive to God.

Fr. Amorth was also insistent on the evil of Yoga. Many exorcists express a lack of understanding of how Yoga really works but say they see many people coming to them with spiritual problems as a result of it. Central to Yoga is a false form of meditation, a channeling of energies, and an opening of the soul to an ambiguous spiritual realm. Independent research about Yoga will demonstrate how even "Christianized" forms of Yoga often still navigate within or alongside a Hindu religious arena, which risks imparting a particular spiritual confusion into the minds of Christians. Since Yoga is so varied in its depth of religious affiliation, some forms are more of an open door than others. However, the risk is the loss of sanctifying grace and possible diabolical influences, which does happen, so the prudential course is to steer clear of it completely.

The Issue of Harry Potter

The books and movies of the popular *Harry Potter* series are known to just about everyone due to the remarkable success of the story. Exorcists have tended to conclude very harshly on the goodness of the story and the soundness of allowing young people to read

---

[28] https://www.irishtimes.com/news/social-affairs/religion-and-beliefs/the-exorcists-bishop-setting-up-team-to-combat-evil-forces-1.3657796

[29] http://www.usccb.org/_cs_upload/8092_1.pdf

[30] Though Hinduism is an established religion, it is a false religion that leads one toward superstition and practices that expose one to the diabolical and is thus also labeled as occult.

it, tending to see it as an opening to curiosity about the occult, if not worse.

In his lectures, Fr. Ripperger provides a lot of important details about the creation and propagation of the occultic fiction books under the title *Harry Potter*. According to Fr. Ripperger, J.K. Rowling, the author of this series of books, went to a witch school before writing the *Harry Potter* series. She wrote the entire series through autowrite, or 'automatic writing,' which is a technique involving demonic assistance. The spells used in the stories are real, as revealed to priests by witches themselves. Exorcists have told him that sixty percent of the names used in the books are the actual names of demons that exorcists have cast out of people.[31]

An exorcist whom Fr. Ripperger knows had to exorcise three children who had simply read the books. Father also mentioned a possession case which involved five demons who claimed that J.K. Rowling was inspired by them to write these books. Fr. Ripperger, and almost all exorcists, tell people to avoid these books. Every time these books are read, which reference the names of demons and, thus, celebrate them, it gives glory to those demons. These books often glorify sin and vice, such as lying and seeking to acquire good through the use of evil.[32]

In an article about Fr. Amorth's comments on Harry Potter, he is quoted as saying, "You start off with Harry Potter, who comes across as a likeable wizard, but you end up with the Devil. There is no doubt that the signature of the Prince of Darkness is clearly within these books."[33] While Fr. Amorth is often quoted as saying it is "not all bad" if the children go and see the movies with their parents, what is not pointed out is that this is because the movies present a much more "toned-down" version of the magical world of Harry Potter. Of course, this would create the illusion that the books are just as safe as the movies, and the parents could be inclined to permit the child to read the books without the supervision of the parents. As Fr. Amorth says, though, particularly after a "soft curiousity" is piqued by viewing the films, "By reading Harry Potter a young child will be drawn

---

[31] Ripperger #1
[32] Ripperger #1
[33] https://www.lifesitenews.com/news/vaticans-chief-exorcist-repeats-condemnation-of-harry-potter-novels

into magic and from there it is a simple step to Satanism and the Devil." Fr. Amorth's quite blunt statement is this: "Behind Harry Potter hides the signature of the king of the darkness, the devil."[34]

It is also known that Pope Benedict, prior to his election to the papacy, expressed his agreement that the *Harry Potter* books were dangerous to the faith of children, as seen in a letter to the German author of a book highly critical of the series. Then-Cardinal Ratzinger is quoting as having written about the "subtle seductions that are barely noticeable and precisely because of that deeply affect (children) and corrupt the Christian faith in souls even before it (the Faith) could properly grow."[35]

Mentioned above was the oft-repeated statement of Fr. Amorth that the *Harry Potter* movies were acceptable, which does not do justice to his criticisms. Similarly, one could look at the comments of Fr. Fortea and, perhaps, come away with a sense that he approves of the book, from a certain perspective. In an interview, he says that he is not in favor of prohibiting the books, seeing that they are just a fantasy story and "unobjectionable." However, in that same interview, noting that children tend to imitate what they see and read, he adds that it is "worrisome that reading these books may lead [children] to attempt the practice of magic or to believe that magic is not as dangerous as their instincts might tell them."[36] As an exorcist, he knows the potential danger which any curiosity about magic could produce.

Exposure to an alluring presentation of magic is dangerous not just for children in this modern age. In an article about the dangers of the *Harry Potter* series, author Michael O'Brien incorporates a statement of Fr. Amorth about the susceptibility of modern man to evil suggestions. He says Fr. Amorth "warns that modern men are losing their sense of the reality of supernatural evil. As a result, he says, many have made themselves more vulnerable to the influence of evil spirits who seek to corrupt and destroy souls."[37]

---

[34] https://www.lifesitenews.com/news/vaticans-chief-exorcist-repeats-condemnation-of-harry-potter-novels

[35] https://www.lifesitenews.com/news/pope-benedict-opposes-harry-potter-novels

[36] https://www.crossroadsinitiative.com/media/articles/interview-with-an-exorcist-fr-jose-antonio-fortea/

[37] https://www.lifesitenews.com/ldn/features/harrypotter/obrienpotter.html

Compendium XI

+ The number of doorways to evil has greatly increased in modern times, and includes evils, like pornography, that have become quite widespread.
+ The statistics regarding the rise in consultation with the occult across the globe are startling.
+ Popular culture and society have become very open and curious about mystical, occultic, and diabolical things, which presents a grave danger, particularly to the youth.
+ Satanism is now in a position where it feels welcomed and entitled to its share of public space and the public forum.
+ The number and variety of New Age practices are also on the increase and pose a serious threat to those in spiritually vulnerable situations.
+ Popular practices, like Yoga, and popular literature, like *Harry Potter*, are clear examples of how entrenched the occult has become in modern society.

Conclusion

There are many questions that we should all be considering as we continue this pilgrimage to eternity. Did someone practice magic in the house I now live in? Is there a witch living in my neighborhood? Am I in a state of mortal sin? Did I pick up any deep wounds to my soul in the years of my past when I lived in sin? Is my house blessed? Who owned my car before me and did any evil happen inside it? Have I had my car blessed? Do I regularly do anything that exposes me to diabolical activity or influences? Do I completely adhere to the teachings of the Church or have I modified those teachings to suit my own desires? Does my family live in accordance with the authority structure that God has willed for it? Do I bless my children regularly? Do I use the sacramentals, like holy water, blessed salt, and blessed oil, to renew the blessing of the Church upon my house? Do I wear a Scapular and abide by the promises I made in its regard? Do I engage in mental prayer on a regular basis? Do I pray daily, as justice requires me to do? Do I ever allow myself to remain in a state of mortal sin without seeking Confession as soon as possible? Have I dabbled in the occult in the past and not brought that up in Confession?

These questions are crucial to ensuring you are not under any deception of the evil one, and to protect your spiritual life, allowing it to grow and flourish. When we treat God as a light issue and a small matter, we prevent Him from imparting His blessings to us. When we refuse to let Him fully into our lives, or push Him away by our deeds, we prevent Him from protecting us from the evils of this world. The Church has offered, by God's inspiration and according to His will, countless and, today, an untold number of blessings and sacramentals that the faithful should eagerly seek out. These blessings are forgotten by most Catholics, and rarely preached by most priests, even those who appear to be very traditional. Regardless of the reason behind this grave oversight, these blessings are in the life of the Church, and the faithful do obtain real positive benefits from their use.

The teachings of experienced priests and exorcists shed tremendous light on our spiritual battles, and their insights are critical to understanding an aspect of our lives that is invisible and craftily hidden. May Our Lord illuminate our intellects and open our wills to conform us more perfectly to what He teaches and bestows upon us through our Holy Mother, the Church. May our journey through this book leave us convicted regarding the work that is before us, and the spiritual weapons that are available to us, as we fight against the invisible forces who work for our damnation.

I conclude here with the words of Saint Paul:

"Finally, be strong in the Lord and in the strength of his might. Put on the whole armor of God, that you may be able to stand against the wiles of the devil. For we are not contending against flesh and blood, but against the principalities, against the powers, against the world rulers of this present darkness, against the spiritual hosts of wickedness in the heavenly places. Therefore take the whole armor of God, that you may be able to withstand in the evil day, and having done all, to stand. Stand therefore, having girded your loins with truth, and having put on the breastplate of righteousness, and having shod your feet with the equipment of the gospel of peace; above all taking the shield of faith, with which you can quench all the flaming darts of the evil one. And take the helmet of salvation, and the sword of the Spirit, which is the word of God. Pray at all times in the Spirit, with all prayer and supplication."[1]

---

[1] Ephesians 6:10-18

References

The prayer in the Appendix, used with permission, comes from a book published by Fr. Ripperger, called <u>Deliverance Prayers: For Use by the Laity</u>. It is available on Amazon in paperback and in Kindle edition. It contains many excellent prayers that address the spiritual needs of the faithful, such as many of those discussed in this book. It is an invaluable resource and a must-have for serious Catholics today.

The following are the spiritual conferences, articles, and books which served as the sources of the teachings of the many exorcists cited in this book.

Talks by Fr. Chad Ripperger

1. "Conference on Exorcism – Fr. Ripperger"
   https://www.youtube.com/watch?v=Ffe_p6kKXqw
   Nov 19, 2013
2. "Fr. Chad Ripperger – Spiritual Warfare Conference – Demons and Possession"
   https://www.youtube.com/watch?v=WiLDxPf0vBg
   Nov 5, 2015
3. "Spiritual Theology Series: Demons (Part 1) ~ Fr. Ripperger"
   https://www.youtube.com/watch?v=v33wu9lPOlE
   July 14, 2018
4. "Spiritual Theology Series: Demons (Part 2) ~ Fr. Ripperger"
   https://www.youtube.com/watch?v=wGi9ZQ21sTQ
   July 14, 2018
5. "Spiritual Warfare Conference 1: Angels & Demons ~ Fr. Ripperger"
   https://www.youtube.com/watch?v=nt_eTbkrR-g
   March 9, 2018
6. "Spiritual Warfare Pt. 1 - Exorcist Fr. Chad Ripperger"
   https://www.youtube.com/watch?v=AiYh96TrITE
   June 6, 2015

7. "Spiritual Warfare Pt. TWO - Exorcist Fr. Chad Ripperger"
   https://www.youtube.com/watch?v=uJc6WGOwtsQ&t=3s
   June 7, 2015
8. "Generational Spirits Conference: Part 1 Introduction ~ Fr. Chad Ripperger"
   https://www.youtube.com/watch?v=-OVhMBuhFo8
   Mar 12, 2017
9. "Generational Spirits Conference: Part 2 Discernment - Fr. Chad Ripperger"
   https://www.youtube.com/watch?v=m1NZovyfad0
   Mar 12, 2017
10. "Generational Spirits 3/3~ Fr. Ripperger"
    https://www.youtube.com/watch?v=ZDpMfT5Way8
    Mar 10, 2017
11. "Levels of Spiritual Warfare ~ Fr. Ripperger"
    https://www.youtube.com/watch?v=TMcvZaiBwe4
    Nov 12, 2018

Talks by Fr. Gary Thomas

1. Fr. Gary Thomas – Interview
   https://www.youtube.com/watch?v=I_wbro4KGZQ
   July 17, 2015
2. Fr. Gary Thomas – Presentation: Exorcist Tells His Story
   https://www.youtube.com/watch?v=PV4FpKX5HNU
   March 18, 2013
3. Fr. Gary Thomas – On the Freemasons
   https://www.youtube.com/watch?v=V5X3fXIGVX8
   January 16, 2018

Talk by Fr. Jeffrey Grob

1. Fr. Jeffrey Grob – Talk About Exorcism at UIC
   https://www.youtube.com/watch?v=lPs8ExKc8fs
   St. John Paul II Newman Center
   Published on Nov 28, 2016

Video with Fr. Cesar Truqui

1. Inside Story: The Ministry of an Exorcist – EWTN Vaticano Special
   https://www.youtube.com/watch?v=pHDjVPKi0QU
   April 6, 2018

Interview with Fr. Randall Weber

1. The Catholic Rite of Exorcism, the Diocesan Exorcist Speaks
   https://www.youtube.com/watch?v=Bv_0gRjUuFo
   Joan Jerkovich Show. March 10, 2012

Talk by Fr. Carlos Martins

1. Exorcism Discussion with Fr. Carlos Martins
   https://www.youtube.com/watch?v=18pg4ugjMoE
   March 14, 2011

Articles referenced:
1. Fr. Piero Catalano
   a. Fr. Piero Catalano article by Gelsomino Del Guercio, for Aleteia.org, from an interview originally published by the *Corriere Della Sera*, Dec. 2017, by Antonio Crispino.
   https://aleteia.org/2018/02/14/padre-pio-is-often-with-me-during-exorcisms-and-the-devil-fears-him/
2. Fr. Gary Thomas
   a. https://www.catholic.com/magazine/print-edition/interview-with-an-exorcist (acc. 7/26/2019)
3. Fr. Jose Fortea
   a. http://www.ncregister.com/daily-news/halloween-the-catholic-faith-and-the-occult (acc. 7/26/2019)
4. Fr. Jeffrey Grob
   a. https://adoremus.org/2018/01/14/understanding-exorcism-interview-father-jeffrey-grob-specialist-rite-exorcism/

5. Msgr. Esseff
    a. http://www.ncregister.com/blog/armstrong/exorcist-says-this-problem-is-far-worse-than-satan (6/15/2019)
6. Fr. Cesar Truqui
    a. https://cruxnow.com/global-church/2017/10/28/exorcist-says-theres-demon-targets-family/
7. Fr. Carlos Martins
    a. http://www.courageouspriest.com/warning-attempt-exorcism-home (accessed 7/23/2019)
    b. https://www.catholicsun.org/2019/02/10/theres-plenty-in-a-name-especially-the-one-that-is-above-every-name/

Books

Amorth, Fr. Gabriele. *An Exorcist Explains the Demonic*. Sophia Institute Press, Manchester, 2016. (footnoted as "Amorth")

Amorth, Fr. Gabriele. *An Exorcist Tells His Story*. Ignatius Press, San Francisco, 1999. (footnoted as "Amorth, *Exorcist Tells*")

Amorth, Fr. Gabriele. *An Exorcist: More Stories*. Ignatius Press, San Francisco, 2002. (footnoted as "Amorth, *More Stories*")

Blai, Adam. *Hauntings, Possessions, and Exorcisms*. Emmaus Road Publishing, Steubenville, 2017.

Carlin, Fr. Paolo. *An Exorcist Explains How to Heal the Possessed*. Sophia Institute Press, Manchester, 2017.

Fortea, Fr. Jose Antonio. *Interview with an Exorcist*. Ascension Press, West Chester, 2006.

Glenn, Msgr. Paul J. *A Tour of the Summa*. TAN Books, Rockford, 1978.

The Roman Ritual. SanctaMissa.org and EWTN.com (accessed August 1, 2019)

The Raccolta. http://www.liturgialatina.org/raccolta and https://archive.org/details/theraccoltaorcol00unknuoft/page/n6 (accessed August 1, 2019)

St. Alphonsus Liguori, and Rev. Robert A. Coffin. *The Glories of Mary.* Ascetical Works, Vol. VII. Charlotte: Tan Books, 2012.

St. Alphonsus Liguori. *Preparation for Death.* Ascetical Works, Vol. I, Grimm Ed., 1926.

St. Alphonsus Liguori. *The True Spouse of Christ.* Ascetical Works, Vol. X, Grimm Ed., 1888. Accessed via https://archive.org.

St. Francis de Sales. *Introduction to the Devout Life.* CCEL https://www.ccel.org/ccel/desales/devout_life.pdf (accessed August 1, 2019)

St. John of the Cross. *Dark Night of the Soul.* CCEL https://www.ccel.org/ccel/john_cross/dark_night.pdf (accessed August 1, 2019)

St. Louis de Montfort. *True Devotion to the Blessed Virgin Mary.* Montfort Publications, New York, 1996.

St. Louis de Montfort, *Hymns.* http://www.montfort.org/content/uploads/pdf/PDF_EN_85_1.pdf (accessed August 1, 2019)

St. Teresa of Avila. *The Life of Teresa of Jesus.* http://www.carmelitemonks.org/Vocation/teresa_life.pdf (accessed August 1, 2019)

Sermons of St. Alphonsus Liguori, 4th Edition, Tan Books, Rockford, 1982.

Additional Resources

Summa Theologiae of St. Thomas
 http://www.newadvent.org/summa/index.html
 (accessed August 1, 2019)

Catena Aurea and Gospel Commentaries of St. Thomas
 https://dhspriory.org/thomas/
 (accessed August 1, 2019)

Appendix

Consecration of One's Exterior Goods to the Blessed Virgin Mary

I, (Name), a faithless sinner, renew and ratify today in thy hands the vows of my Baptism; I renounce forever Satan, his pomps and works; and I give myself entirely to Jesus Christ, the Incarnate Wisdom, to carry my cross after Him all the days of my life, and to be more faithful to Him than I have ever been before. In the presence of all the heavenly court, I choose thee, O Mary, this day for my Mother and Mistress. Knowing that I have received rights over all my exterior goods by the promulgation of the Natural Law by the Divine Author, I deliver and consecrate to thee, as thy slave, all of my exterior goods, past, present and future; I relinquish into thy hands, my Heavenly Mother, all rights over my exterior goods, including my health, finances, relationships, possessions, property, my job and my earthly success and I retain for myself no right of disposing the goods that come to me but leave to thee the entire and full right of disposing of all that belongs to me, without exception, according to thy good pleasure, for the greater glory of God in time and in eternity. As I now interiorly relinquish what belongs to me exteriorly into thy hands, I entrust to thee the protection of those exterior goods against the evil one, so that, knowing that they now belong to thee, he cannot touch them. Receive, O good and pious Virgin, this little offering of what little is, in honor of, and in union with, that subjection which the Eternal Wisdom deigned to have to thy maternity; in homage to the power which both of you have over this poor sinner, and in thanksgiving for the privileges with which the Holy Trinity has favored thee. Trusting in the providential care of God the Father and thy maternal care, I have full confidence that thou wilst take care of me as to the necessities of this life and will not leave me forsaken. God the Father, increase my trust in Thy Son's Mother; Our Lady of Fair Love, give me perfect confidence in the providence of Thy Son. Amen.[1]

---

[1] From "Deliverance Prayers: For Use by the Laity" by Fr. Chad Ripperger, on Amazon.

About the Author

Charles D. Fraune was the founding Theology teacher of Christ the King Catholic High School in Huntersville, NC and has been a Theology teacher there for eight years. In addition, he has taught nearly every grade level, from second grade to adult, including on the college and Diocesan level. He spent three semesters in seminary with the Diocese of Raleigh at St. Charles Borromeo Seminary in Pennsylvania. This completed a nine-year discernment of the priesthood and religious life after which he discerned that Our Lord was not calling him to the priesthood. He has a Master of Arts in Theology from the Christendom College Graduate School, as well as an Advanced Apostolic Catechetical Diploma. His enjoyment of writing began over twenty years ago, and finally culminated in his first completed book, *Come Away By Yourselves*. In addition to this, he has been working on books related to various aspects of the Catholic Faith, and to the powerful story of his return to the Catholic Faith after a time struggling with illness and depression. Charles is also a dedicated "backyard farmer." He lives in the Diocese of Charlotte, NC with his wife and three young children.

To our readers

We would like to hear from our readers.

Comments, questions, suggested topics for additional books, etc.

Please send your email to CharlesFraune@TheRetreatBox.com.

Keep up with spiritual warfare news, commentaries, and publications at our website: www.TheSlayingDragonsBook.com.